VISIBLE LIGHT

Also by Michael Lesy

Wisconsin Death Trip
Real Life
Time Frames
Bearing Witness

VISIBLE LIGHT

MICHAEL LESY

Photographs by
Angelo Rizzuto,
William Burke,
John McWilliams,
and Andrea Kovács

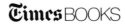 BOOKS

1985

Copyright © 1985 by Michael Lesy

All rights reserved under International and
Pan-American Copyright Conventions.
Published in the United States by Times Books,
a division of Random House, Inc., New York,
and simultaneously in Canada by Random
House of Canada Limited, Toronto.

Photographs by Andrea Kovács copyright
© 1985 by Andrea Kovács
Photographs by William Burke copyright
© 1980, 1981, 1985 by William Burke
Photographs by John McWilliams copyright
© by John McWilliams

Library of Congress Cataloging in Publication Data

Lesy, Michael, 1945–
    Visible light.

    1. Photographers—Biography.   I. Title.
TR139.L47   1985   770′.92′2 [B]   84–40428
ISBN 0-8129-1156-3 (hardcover)
ISBN 0-8129-1305-1 (paperback)

Designed by Betty Binns Graphics/Martin Lubin

Manufactured in the United States of America

9 8 7 6 5 4 3 2
First Edition

To Liz, Nadia, and Alex

ACKNOWLEDGMENTS

For his friendship: Roger Straus III. For their critical insights: Eileen Berger, Aristide Caratzas, David Horwath, Kent Stephens, and Jeremy Zwelling. For his hospitality: Eugene Richards. For their advice and affection: Hope McGowan, Susan Rosenberg, Ilene Segalove, and Julie D. Taylor. For their time and information: Jerry Maddox, James Montgomery, Frank Rizzuto, Catherine Vescio, and Ted Wathen. For their assistance: Cathy Roberts and JoAnn Stephens.

This book was conceived in response to the art of Minor White and the thought of Susan Sontag.

The people in this book seem to have little in common. One had an ancestor who was shipwrecked, blown ashore, and robbed of his clothes by Indians, 150 years before the Revolution; another is the daughter of an exiled political hero who hid from the Nazis and ran from the Communists. There's one whose father was a cookie salesman and another whose father made a fortune serving a company that used its workers like hammers. One was an anti-Semite; another is a Jew. One was a recluse; another roamed the continent. All are photographers, but their pictures couldn't be more different: One made cityscapes; another made portraits in little towns. One made landscapes; another did nothing for years but photograph her own skin. There's one whose camera produced negatives as big as this page and as finely detailed as etchings, and another who bought her equipment in a drugstore.

What they have in common are lives that read like parables whose instruments of grace and means of revelation are cameras. There's the story of one man so fearfully damaged by life that in another age he might have become a hermit. Instead, he used a camera to carry himself out into the world and then to rise so high above it that he began to believe he was an angel. There's the story of another so painfully marked when he was young that when he grew up, he traveled to a place full of people so marked by other fates that the photographs he made of them became talismans against his own despair. In the end, instead of becoming an angel, he walked into a church and was anointed by a priest. There's the story of a third man who stood under a bridge and had a prophetic vision. Because of it, he abandoned everything and traveled everywhere, looking for it again. Whenever he saw it, he took a picture of it. And there's the story of a woman who used a camera to record her neuroses, her cure, and her religious rebirth, a ten-year process chronicled by photographs made first as forms of therapy, then as means of meditation, finally as evidence of her own transcendence.

None of the people in this book is, at this moment in the history of art and photography, particularly famous. One died in obscurity; the others were lucky enough to have attended the best schools and to have had their share of prestigious fellowships and commissions, but none has had his or her brow wreathed with laurels or an obituary published in *The New York Times.* They are, in other words, honorable members of a particular profession, accomplished but not celebrated, neither as eminent as soloists nor as obscure as members of the chorus. They all are people who persisted in their vision. To understand why they persisted may also be to understand the motives of many, many others who, like them, stand halfway between fame and anonymity.

Cameras have often been described as the equivalents of pencils: simple, common devices that can write invoices as well as sonnets, songs as well as threatening letters. Some intellectuals have dismissed photography as a form of sublimated murder and unconsummated rape. Some artists and curators have spoken of it as a descriptive fiction whose form is its only content. Photography may be any and all of these things, but if the lives of the people in this book are to be believed and if, in some fashion, they resemble the lives of others, then photography has become, in this part of the century, a powerful autobiographical medium—a medium that, advertently and inadvertently, reveals the private minds of its practitioners: photographs as projections of private predicaments; subjects as masks that precisely fit their viewers' faces. The woman, in this book, who photographed herself and used those photographs to reveal and restore herself to herself may have known what she was doing. But the damaged man who thought he was an angel actually believed he was photographing the world instead of keeping a diary, and the man who sought out and photographed others who wore on their faces the marks he carried in his heart would only reluctantly have admitted that he was making surrogate self-portraits. As for the man who had a vision while standing underneath a bridge, he believed he was a prophet until one day he realized he was only hiding behind his camera.

For better or for worse, all the people in this book reached for a camera at a certain moment in their lives the way someone with asthma reaches for an inhaler. None of the people in this book began to make photographs because it was either socially useful or artful or profitable. To say they did it for their own clarity of mind isn't enough. They did it, whether they knew it or not, to save and heal their own souls.

CONTENTS

One: The Angel   **3**

Two: The Driver   **37**

Three: The Sailor   **83**

Four: The Convert   **131**

VISIBLE LIGHT

In 1967 a recluse who called himself the Little Angel died in New York and left 60,000 photographs and $50,000 to the Library of Congress, on the condition that the library publish a book of his work—a book that he had never completed. The library dutifully published a booklet bound with staples, illustrated with perhaps sixty indifferently printed reproductions of the dead man's pictures. It then proceeded to spend his money. But instead of spending it all on typewriters and paper clips, it began to buy the work of some of the most eminent and innovative photographers of the nineteenth and twentieth centuries. At auctions, it acquired the calotypes of such early practitioners of the medium as David Octavius Hill and Robert Adamson; from dealers it purchased the portfolios of such twentieth-century American artists as Diane Arbus and Duane Michals. The library took the dead man's money and turned it into a collection of master photographers. What it did with his prints was to store them in the subbasement of an annex, where it left them, along with countless others, stacked like bones in an ossuary, to suffer the benign neglect of optimum temperature and humidity.

Years after the recluse had died and left his burden to the library, a curator showed me his images. How I came to be there is a story without linear sense. When I was young, I was sent to a series of private schools that served as cold storage lockers in which the sons of a regional version of the rich, the wellborn, and the able were kept at a temperature low enough to prevent spoilage but high enough to maintain circulation. It was thought that young men would emerge from such places in good enough condition to enter the best finishing and professional schools. Until that time they were kept on ice to prevent them from doing themselves damage. Occasionally some of them would grow restless and come awake. They would look around uneasily, trying to understand how they came to be in such a cold and quiet place. But since there was nothing to see except other sleepers and since the air was so chill and silent, they would soon go back to sleep.

One afternoon, when I was fourteen, I woke up for some reason. I walked down an empty street, through an arched corridor of old elms, into a building that was both a church and a library. On the upper floor was a Georgian chapel; on the ground floor were alcoves lined with books. One of these alcoves was a narrow vaulted room, twenty feet high, its entrance barred by a wrought iron gate. For some reason, every time I awoke, I walked to that building and went to that alcove, but each time I found it locked. This time its gate was ajar. I pulled it wide and went in. There was an oak table in the room, and shelves that went up to the ceiling. On the shelves were hundreds of volumes, each the same size, each bound in red. I pulled one out with both hands and read its title. It said *Life.* I opened it and looked inside. It was filled with pictures of an entire world I had never seen, either asleep or awake. There were unrecognizable cars, cigarettes, and women wearing lingerie. In the middle of it was a picture I couldn't understand. It grew larger as I looked at it. It appeared as if hundreds of people were lying on a huge flight of stairs, sleeping on top of one another. They were dressed all in gray. There were so many of them that if someone had wanted to come down the stairs, he would have had to step on them. They were lying in such awkward positions, in such a tangle, in such a strange and uncomfortable place that I wondered how they could stay asleep. Then I read the caption. They were Chinese civilians, and they all were dead. I closed the volume, walked back to my room, and fell asleep again.

Seven years went by until I saw another photograph. By then I was a student at Columbia University. I had just learned how to use a camera. It was a device called a range finder that had a little window through which I could look at the world. Whenever I did, I saw two of everything; one was the subject, and the other its double, cast in amber light. In order to take a picture, I turned a ring so that the double fused with its original. Then I pressed a button and heard a beautiful, brushed chrome click.

While I was learning to do this, I was enrolled in a class whose research assignments allowed me a temporary pass into the stacks of the university library. Outside, around the upper edge of the building, were the names of authors, savants, scientists, and philosophers carved in stone. Inside were stacks so intricate and endless tht the entire human race could have found sanctuary there. One morning I showed my pass and climbed the steps to a place where I had discovered books of Greek lyric poetry. For some reason, when I got there, I didn't stop but kept climbing. I opened a door, turned down a corridor, found another door onto another flight, and went up, finding other doors and other corridors until I stood in a large empty room whose floor was of stone and whose walls were lined with map cases. The cases contained nineteenth-century scenic engravings, turned facedown, stored in no apparent order. I turned them over quickly, making eddies in the stale and dusty air. At some moment in this idle process I suddenly came face-to-face with an old man, his head covered with a black velvet cap, surrounded by darkness. His white hair rose like flames around his cap; his forehead was lined like a plowed field; his eyebrows were as thick and white as hedges covered with ice. But it was his eyes, eyes that must have been pale blue when he was alive, that stared out and up at me, amazed, stunned, and astonished. Neither he nor I had expected to meet. He had been face-

down in the drawer for seventy years, long after Julia Margaret Cameron, his friend, had taken his picture in 1867. For seventy years he had been wildly staring at nothing but the back of an engraving. And now he was staring at me as if I, not he, were the ghost. Years later I learned that he was Sir John Hershel, the chemist, the son of Sir William, the astronomer. It was Sir John who had invented a way to fix permanently the fleeting images made by silver salts, exposed to the sun. It was he who had first spoken of a photographic positive and negative and had prophesied the snapshot. Years later I learned all this, but at the time I first saw him and he saw me, I felt like a man who had brought the dead back to life with a glance. For it was I who had found him and returned his gaze and, by returning it, had given light back to his eyes. I stared at him until that light diminished. Then I turned him back over and left the room.

For another seven years I studied history and practiced photography until, one day, the two fused like the images in my first range finder. I came to believe that photographs were both aesthetic objects *and* forms of data which revealed what was real and what was imagined to be real. For the next ten years I traveled from one place to another, looking through archives that contained nothing but photographs, searching through collections of images, piecing together a collage made of books, whose recurrent subject was love and death. Over the years I began to notice something strange about the photographic curators, researchers, editors, and teachers I met in the course of my investigations. It seemed as if the best of them had suffered a common occupational disease, almost as if they had been workers exposed to an industrial toxin. Yet the disease they suffered seemed not to shorten their lives but to prolong them. It seemed to me that those who exposed themselves every day to the sight and intense study of photographs experienced a prolonged youth and a retarded old age, as if each one of them were Dorian Gray. I met curators of sixty who had gray hair but the eyes of boys, and others, in their fifties, who had the complexions and shyness of adolescents. I met middle-aged researchers who had long ago married and borne children but who conducted themselves with the animated grace of young girls. I came to know wizened teachers of photography who lived on cigarettes and coffee but who, from a distance of twenty feet, looked like young punks. I heard stories of others who capered about in their last years like children trying on faces. Of course, there were a few who looked and acted their ages, but the ones who seemed younger than their years were also the ones who had been studying photographs (and often practicing photography) longer and more intensely than the others.

I came to believe that such people retarded the effects of time not simply because of the sedentary and contemplative nature of their profession but because of the very objects they studied and the way in which they studied them. I began to imagine that within every photograph, no matter how banal or remarkable, an essential element of time had been encapsulated, embodied by a glance or a gesture which was never finished but was always begun again each time it was activated by the onlooker's attention. It seemed to me that this encapsulated time, combined with the onlooker's insight, retarded the normal course of age. I began to think of it as a process in stages: Every investigator began by observing the image before him. The image was inevitably an appearance of action or emotion without fruition, a peak moment held in abeyance. There were some observers who looked at an image just long enough to recognize and comprehend it. But there were others who passed beyond this intellectual understanding into a state of imaginative projection and amazement. During this state they were drawn into the significant details they had earlier comprehended. It was during this time that they began vicariously to participate in the incomplete moment before their eyes. This projective state of mind (which had to have been preceded by an intellectual comprehension) activated and then reactivated whatever unfinished gesture or glance was recorded, and it was this reactivation that drew such onlookers still deeper into the encapsulated moment. In this way they took leave of the time kept by the clocks and calendars of their contemporaries and entered the appearance of time past. Time, lived within visual fragments, kept them young.

Whether or not the study of photographs was actually a fountain of youth, I was certain they contained allusive information about the past that conventional, written forms of historical data did not. Photographs looked as if they were replicas when in fact they were metaphors; they appeared to be records of actuality when they were frequently allegories; they seemed to display a few simple truths when, as often as not, they were paradoxes. Conventional historians, who had enough trouble reading between the lines of diplomatic cables, kept a safe distance from such chimeras. The few who weren't afraid of too many questions and who spent their time reading and rereading the primary data as intently and critically as if they were talmudists called themselves revisionists. I met one once—a historian of foreign policy—who had strayed so far from the sculpted footnotes of secondary sources that he had arrived at a new set of explanations for everything from the annexation of Texas to the war in Vietnam. He used to give his explanations in public, in front of large numbers of college sophomores. The sons of a major publisher of textbooks had been his students; during vacation they had gone home and told their father about the man who had all the answers. The old man, who had begun to have doubts about Vietnam, asked the historian to write a new version of the American past, suitable for survey courses. Eventually the historian asked me to unearth photographs that would not simply illustrate his chapters but promote speculation among his readers. It was in the course of that research that I found myself sitting at a crowded table in the Prints and Photographs Division of the Library of Congress, asking a middle-aged curator, who stooped and stammered like a kid with growing pains, whether he had any photographs from the fifties. He went to look, and when he came back, he was rolling a loaded mail cart. Its trays were stuffed with the lifework of Angelo Rizzuto, the recluse.

Standing upright in the cart were folders crammed with eight- by ten-inch contact sheets. On every sheet were 36 pictures, each picture one and a half inches long and one inch high, every sheet the equivalent of a single roll of 36-exposure, 35 mm, black-and-white film. There were hundreds and hundreds of the sheets. Tens of thousands of pictures. All in miniature. I had never before seen that many contact sheets. I looked at the first one. It was dated and numbered "May 1952, #1." I picked my way to the last: "July 1966, #7." They all were like that: month, year, and film roll number. Fifteen years of them. A dated record. From Eisenhower nearly to Nixon. Perhaps 60,000 pictures, printed in a form in which one frame followed another in the essential order of its original exposure. Years ago Henri Cartier-Bresson, the master documentary photographer, talked of contact sheets as privileged information, since, at a glance, they revealed the visual thinking of the photographer: the way in which he first saw a subject, approached it, closed toward it, and finally fused its form and content in his frame. To read the frame progressions of the contact sheet of a master photographer was like watching a man drive a nail into wood: the first tentative taps to establish a rhythm, a reach, and a placement; the next few to confirm them; and then the last rapid power strokes to drive it deep. Stuffed in the cart in front of me that morning were not just thousands of images made by one man but the schematic traces of thousands of his visual thoughts, the result of countless interactions between his curiosity and entrancement and what the world was and appeared to be. The sheets were the graphic equivalent of electroencephalograms; the question was whether the man's brain had had any significant thoughts.

To begin with, the sheets were evidence of a conscientious and orderly mind. Not only were they dated, but they had, in fact, been made. For although the process of developing a roll of film, inspecting the negatives, cutting them into nine-inch strips, laying the strips on top of a piece of photo paper beneath a piece of glass, and then briefly illuminating them to contact-print them is a simple process that provides a valuable record, it is often performed by photographers (who invariably like to shoot more than to print) with as much en-thusiasm as children brushing their teeth every night or gardeners weeding their vegetables. The man who made the hundreds of contact sheets stuffed in the mail cart appeared to have performed this drudgery every day for years. It seemed, however, that he had often been hasty, and sometimes careless: Many of the sheets still smelled of the fixer, hyposulfate, as if they had not been thoroughly washed, and many were warped and bent, as if they had not been left long enough to dry flat in a place of uniform heat and humidity. On some of the sheets some of his exposures were out of focus either because he hadn't focused his camera or because he hadn't pressed his negatives flush with the photo paper beneath the glass when he contact-printed them. Also, on many of the sheets there were often a few frames that were either too dark or too light to read—the result of negatives with densities considerably thicker or thinner than those of others on the sheet, as if he had regularly moved from places and subjects in bright light to ones in deep shadow. In spite of these deficiencies, there were so many adequate exposures and so many well-dated and ordered contact sheets that their gaps were no more disturbing than the lapses in a long diary.

I began to scan the sheets, looking at their subjects. I had no magnifying glass, but most of the frames that were clear enough could be read at a glance. I started a list. By the end of the day it had turned

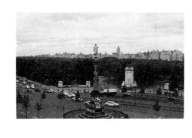 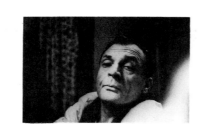 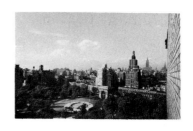

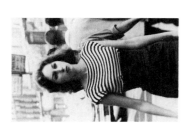 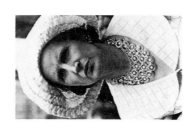 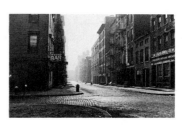

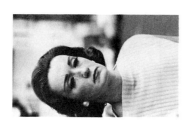 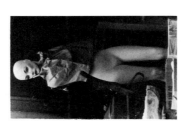 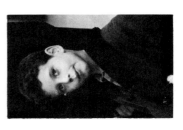

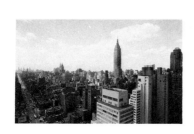 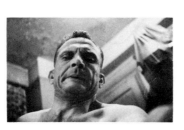 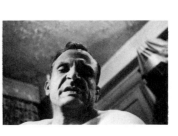

into a prose poem: streetfights, bums, and sideshows; cityscapes seen from above; statues, cats, and sleeping children; men talking and men reading; circus acrobats, sleepers, Sunday painters, and couples arguing; skaters, lovers, cooks, vendors, parks, graveyards, little boys alone, and women walking; subway riders, mannequins, and movie marquees; taxis, street preachers, speakers, and sign painters; drunks, self-portraits, street festivals, and dead men; empty streets and scratched-out pictures; nuns, dogs, fat men, and statues; more cityscapes and more self-portraits; Hasidim, junkmen, and parades; little girls and women of all ages; cops and grotesques. The imagery seemed so dense and pungent that I stopped thinking about the historical research I was there to conduct and began to think about the man and the pictures he had made.

It seemed that I was looking at the work of a man who had decided to record the whole world. I tried to think of precedents for what he'd done. I thought of the Frenchman Eugène Atget, the former sailor and actor who wandered around Paris at the time of Proust, lugging his big camera, making pictures of streets, gardens, buildings, doorways, and fountains, selling them to clients, but ending up bent and grizzled, dressed in a black overcoat, living on bits of bread soaked in milk. The man whose work I had seen had not lived as long as Atget, and there was no evidence he had any clients.

Then I thought of the photographic surveys made of America in the thirties by the Farm Security Administration (FSA). They had been directed by an economics instructor named Roy Stryker, who had become a government bureaucrat and then hired such photographers as Walker Evans, Dorothea Lange, and Russell Lee. All these photographers traveled into the world alone, but if they needed it, they had Stryker and his office to vouch for them. They all had a place to come back to. And Stryker himself hadn't thought up the project alone: He had read *Middletown,* talked to the Lynds, and been the protégé of Rexford Tugwell, a member of the Roosevelt brain trust. From what little I knew, Rizzuto had had no mentor, and nowhere to come back to, and, from the disparate variety of his images, had no theoretical agenda to guide him in his wanderings.

I tried to recall other precedents; I kept making analogies. There had been Ralph Fasanella, the radical fay naïve artist of life in New York, but except for the pictures of cops and bums, none of Rizzuto's pictures had any political content. And none of them was naïvely crafted. I had seen cityscapes as grandly lit and framed as Canaletto's, and streets as barren and strangely lit as De Chirico's. I remembered one image made in a subway that looked like an Evans from *Many Are Called*; I thought of a family group in a food stand that looked like an image from Robert Frank's *The Americans*; there were shots of

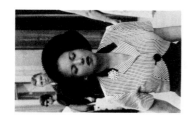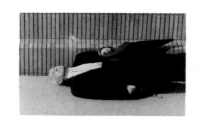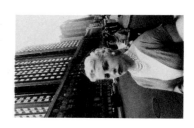

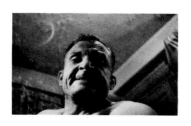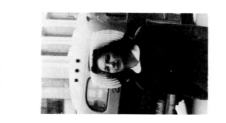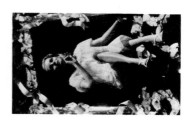

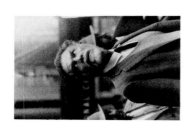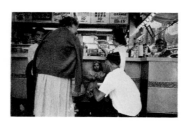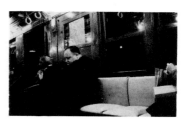

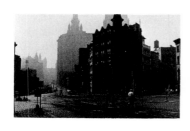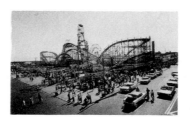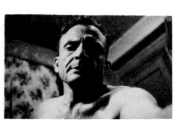

women on the street that resembled the vulnerable and harshly lit portraits that Harry Callahan had made in Chicago; and there were even some frame progressions that were as poetically linked, one to the other, as some of the images in Ralph Gibson's *Déjà-Vu*. When they were seen in one sitting, the repetitive, desperate, and fecund variety of Rizzuto's pictures created a state of mind equivalent to that inspired by the *Tropics* of Henry Miller and Louis Ferdinand Céline's *Death on the Installment Plan*.

But beyond these analogies there were his self-portraits, images made by his holding his camera at arm's length, images of a solitary man who glared, grimaced, and stared down into his own lens. It was the constancy of the self-portraits, the way in which they punctuated the massive cityscapes seen from above, as well as the appearance, again and again, of the images of the Statue of Liberty, the monument to Christopher Columbus, and the urns in front of the Public Library on Forty-second Street that made me wonder if I was looking at an aborted documentary or an allegory. I thought of the story that Jorge Borges once told of a great artist who, when he grew old, decided to paint a vast mural of the entire universe. Borges said that the artist painted the stars in the heavens, the birds of the air, and the monsters of the deep. He painted lovers laughing, mothers with their children, and strong men in their glory. He did this, day after day, until he was too weak to work. Close to death, he drew back from his mural to see it whole for the first time—only to discover that he had painted a portrait of his own face. Perhaps the work I was seeing was like that. Perhaps at some point during his fifteen years of effort, Rizzuto had unconsciously transformed recognizable public places and human types into symbols in a moral tale. Perhaps what had begun as a daily journey with a camera through the city's streets had become for him a Pilgrim's Progress in which the world became a projection of his own solitary predicament.

But why had he done what he'd done? Why had he persisted? To what end? For what reason? How had he survived? I asked the curator, but he was innocent. All he knew was that Rizzuto had been born in South Dakota. In Deadwood, in 1906. He'd been reared in Omaha, gone to a little college in Ohio, and graduated in 1931. Somehow or other, he'd ended up in New York and begun to take pictures. Just before he died, he'd confessed to someone that he was working on a book that would be a visual record of New York, 300 years after it had passed from the Dutch to the English. It was to be modeled after a work entitled *The Iconography of Manhattan Island, 1498–1909,* written by a man named Isaac Newton Phelps Stokes. Rizzuto was going to call his book *Little Old New York* by Anthony Angel. He'd died before he'd finished, and he'd left everything to the Library of Congress. Unfortunately there'd been some sort of nasty lawsuit about the whole thing.

While the curator went to look for documents, I started asking myself a new set of questions: How, in the name of God, had someone named Rizzuto managed to be born in Deadwood? That place was the center of the gold-mining region of the Black Hills. There'd been brothels next to banks on the main street. Custer had been rubbed out, defending the whole operation from the Sioux and the Cheyenne, who thought it was an abomination. To have been born there! And then brought up in Omaha! A place of railroads, beef cattle, stockyards, and bad winters. A place as quick, crooked, and crazy as a river town with tracks instead of water. An Italian in Omaha! From an ambitious family grown rich enough to send him to college when no more than 10 percent of the people went past high school.

The curator came back with a long memorandum. It was dated 1969, addressed to William Ruckelshaus Esq., then assistant attorney general in the civil division of the Justice Department. It was an account of the origin of the lawsuit brought against the estate of Angelo Rizzuto by one of his brothers. The story began with three brothers—Frank, Sam, and Angelo. After their father had died in the thirties, they fought over his estate. Frank and Sam had lived at various times in Denver and Omaha, taking care of the businesses they'd inherited. In 1941 Angelo had gone to Denver to resolve the fight over the estate. While he was there, he tried to kill himself. He was treated in a private sanatorium where he was diagnosed as suffering from "dementia praecox, paranoid type." When he was discharged six months later, he enlisted in the army. Seven months after that he was given an honorable medical discharge. His army and hospital records "indicated that the decedent, Angelo Rizzuto, was suffering paranoid delusions concerning his two brothers and other powerful forces, including railroads, lawyers, Jews, and unidentified big businesses." He believed his brothers and those other forces were cheating him out of his rightful inheritance.

Nothing more is known of him again until 1959, when his older brother Frank died without a will. Then Angelo started writing letters to the attorney for the administrator of Frank's estate and to many others, including state legislators and judges. He sent copies of his letters to the U.S. attorney general, the FBI, and the internal security division of the Justice Department. "Decedent, on a number of occasions, expressed his belief that Frank's estate was dominated by insane judges of the Denver courts and by Communists, in and out of local government. There is little question that decedent suffered from an insane delusion with respect to Communists and perverts in government." After he died in 1967 and left his estate to the Library of Congress, his brother Sam claimed that he lacked "testamentary capacity." Sam charged that Angelo "was suffering an insane delusion" that Sam was cheating him out of his money. By the time the case was settled out of court Sam himself had died.

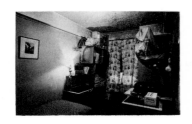 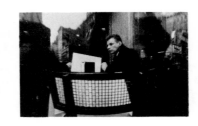 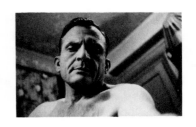

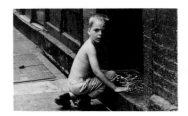 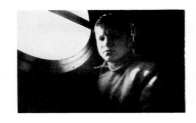 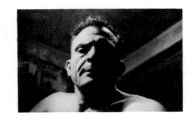

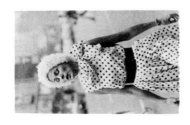 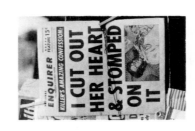 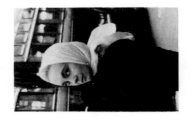

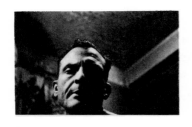 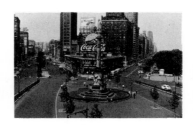 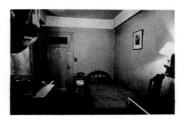

After the attorneys had been paid, Sam's estate was awarded one-fourth of Angelo's. The library kept the rest.

As I read this, the image of Rizzuto as an American Atget disappeared from my mind, replaced by a man who could have been invented by Nikolai Gogol. It was all in the pictures: the self-portraits; the scratched-out frames; the interior shots of the narrow room he must have rented from month to month for fifteen years in a hotel—the door and the house phone; a single bed pushed against a wall; a large desk with a shrouded enlarger on it pushed against the other wall; one window, covered with drapes of floral nightmare; a sink but no toilet; a ceiling with plaster so rotten that it looked like the roof of a cave. In this room he developed his film, made his contact sheets, and slept. The only decoration was a handsomely framed print of the wall of a courtyard; the only evidence of pleasure, an old portable radio. And in the corner were a tiny desk, where he wrote his crazy letters, and shelves, stacked with packages of photographs—photographs made by a paranoid who suspected Communists, perverts, and Jews but who spent the last fifteen years of his life living in and documenting a city that had not only more Jews than Jerusalem but more radicals and deviants than the states of Nebraska and South Dakota had Italians.

The only problem with turning what remained of him into a madman with a camera was his contact sheets. The same ones that revealed his anguish, his isolation, and—when I looked again, I saw—his rage revealed a man entranced with the compositional clarity of rectilinear space on a massive scale seen from on high. His sheets were dotted not only with grand cityscapes and architectural landmarks but with historical markers, and in the years before copy machines they were punctuated by photographs of pages from history books, articles from *Harper's Weekly,* and turn-of-the-century news items from *The New York Times.* Beyond this evidence of a man aware of history and entranced by architecture was his reference to Stokes's *Iconography* as his intellectual model. Stokes was the wrong hero for a madman. He was a patrician, the son of a merchant banker who had been one of the founders of the Metropolitan Museum. Stokes himself had been an eminent architect who had designed such structures as the Baltimore Stock Exchange and St. Paul's Chapel at Columbia but who also, in an act of noblesse oblige, had spent years designing, lobbying for, and building sanitary tenements for New York's working poor. His six-volume *Iconography,* published between 1915 and 1928, had grown out of his own collection of historical prints and views of old New York. The massive work consisted of three volumes of maps, views, and architectural photographs and three volumes of chronicles based on his belief that "the ideal method of presenting history [is] to . . . allow the facts and the myths together with interpretations and . . . even . . . casual comments to speak for themselves." It was an immense collection of visual and written quotation, strung together in chronological order. Its complexity would have better satisfied the curiosity of a historian like Giovanni Battista Vico or a writer like James Joyce than the disordered capacities of a paranoid schizophrenic, released, far from home, on his own recognizance.

I spent another day looking through Rizzuto's contact sheets and making slides of some of them. Then I left and didn't return for four years. Even though I traveled to many other places and studied many other photographs, I kept thinking of what Rizzuto had done and kept wondering why I persisted. Once I told his story and showed his contacts to a group of teachers and scholars of photography. I asked, without having any answers, how it was possible that an obscure recluse who seemed to have had no knowledge of the work of such photographic artists as Walker Evans, Harry Callahan, Robert Frank, Garry Winogrand, and Lee Friedlander could have made images that resembled theirs? Was it that he simply pointed a camera with good optics at a modern city and that because the city was there and because he was competent, persistent, and lucky, he made images whose idioms were in a photographic tradition (once called the new social landscape) of which he was ignorant? How much, I wondered, were the creation and elaboration of such visual idioms the result of individual genius and will, and how much the result of opportunities made available by applied technology and offered by the nature of a common place and predicament in time? Before I was finished, some of the people who were listening grew angry. Either they thought that I was trying to make them believe that Rizzuto was an emperor wearing new clothes when, in fact, he was a naked fool and I was a charlatan, or they thought I was trying to strip true artists of their robes and dress everyone alike.

I left the room that night wondering if I was fooling myself as well as them. Had I become an anarchist playing a joke on the academy? Or had I simply studied too many pictures for too many years and so deadened my sensibilities that only a lunatic with a camera could provoke my curiosity? I sought out a man whose critical intelligence I had often relied upon and showed him the pictures and told him the stories I had told the others. We sat and talked in a room twenty floors above the streets of New York. The photographs of the women, he said, he had hoped they would interest him. But the man who made them was no Jacques Henri Lartigue. As for the cityscapes seen from above—he looked out his window and dismissed them with his hand. Then he changed the subject. He wondered if, in my investigations, I had come upon any collections of atrocity photographs.

I lived with Rizzuto's story a bit longer

after that until something came to me: He was neither Lartigue, the little boy with the camera who loved women, nor was he Evans, nor Callahan, nor any of the others. Perhaps he had come close more than once, but in art, close is not enough. For fifteen years he had used the camera to record himself and his sight of the world with the persistence of a man whose life depended on it. What he claimed he was doing was one thing; what he accomplished was another. He never succeeded in rivaling Stokes's *Iconography,* but in the process he created an inadvertent visual diary. His art may have remained private and obscure, but it was an art based on solitary need. It was this *need* that he had in common with all the others, whether greater fools or masters than he, who picked up a camera and used it to carry themselves, alone, into the world. If I could understand Rizzuto's art, then I could use it to understand the greater art of others, just as some royal courts kept dwarfs the better to see the dignity of their rulers. To do this, I had to discover the origins of Rizzuto's nature. I had to begin the search. So I went to see his executor.

Rizzuto's executor was an attorney named James Montgomery. Montgomery's face, voice, and bearing were those of a man far better bred and educated than his surroundings would indicate. His father's family, he said, had lived in New York for generations. He himself had graduated from Harvard Law School in 1948 and,

after a few years with a firm, had set out on his own, turning last requests into legal instruments called wills. In his early years he had given his name to a referral service operated by the bar association. Sometimes the people referred to him had problems that only God or the devil could solve; other times they became his clients. In June 1967 the service gave his name to Angelo Rizzuto, who called him from Roosevelt Hospital. Rizzuto said he wanted to make a will; he said it was a matter of some urgency. When Montgomery got to the hospital, he met a small, slight man who calmly told him that he was dying of cancer and that he was in a hurry. Rizzuto said he owned two things of value: a house on Fifty-first Street, between First and Second avenues, and a collection of photographs he had made of New York over a period of twenty years. The house was worth (then) perhaps $70,000. When he died, he wanted it sold, and once his debts had been settled—there were $10,000 in back taxes—he wanted his estate to finance the publication of a book of his pictures. Whatever money remained was to be given, along with the photographs, to the Library of Congress. He was unmarried, he said, and his only living relative was a brother, but because they'd fought over an inheritance, he didn't want to leave him a penny. He wanted his next-door neighbor, a man called Peter Sutherland, to be his executor. Montgomery took notes, offered some advice, and told him he'd be back with the will as soon as he could. When he returned a week later, he met Sutherland.

Montgomery said that Sutherland appeared to have been Rizzuto's only friend in the world. He was an unmarried forty-five-year-old man who rented rooms to tenants in the house where he'd been born and where he still lived with his parents. After Rizzuto had died and the will was contested, Sutherland gave a deposition on his behalf. He admitted that he'd always thought Rizzuto a bit peculiar: After he'd moved in, he'd covered all his windows with burlap, and he never went out, except once a day, always at 2:00 P.M., carrying cameras. Sutherland's old mother had admired such regularity as the mark of a man of character. Three years went by. Then Sutherland's old cat got sick and found a place to rest in Rizzuto's backyard. Sutherland braced himself and went over the fence after her. Rizzuto came out; Sutherland said he was sorry; Rizzuto said she was a nice cat; Sutherland apologized again; Rizzuto said he often fed her himself. That sort of conversation went on for two years until the cat died. Then Rizzuto sent Sutherland, who had also suffered the loss of his mother, some memorial pictures of the cat sitting on the fence. Two more years went by without another word, or, as Sutherland said, "We resumed our normal lack of relationship." One winter Sutherland wrote Rizzuto a polite note, asking him please to remove a patch of snow from his sidewalk since, when it melted, the water always ran down and froze again in front of the rooming house where it threatened the life of an old lady with a bad leg. Rizzuto said he'd be happy to help.

After that there was, said Sutherland, "a subtle happening"; people began to notice that Rizzuto was losing a lot of weight. That spring he called Sutherland to tell him he was in the hospital; "he just wanted to assure me that the gas had been shut off, that he was an ill man, and he just wanted me not to worry if he wasn't there. . . ." Soon he called again. He was back home, and if Mr. Sutherland had a minute, would he mind stopping by? Sutherland hadn't been next door in twenty years. He got there the same time as the delivery boy from the drugstore. Rizzuto came to the door, wearing pajamas and carrying some sort of bag, connected to a tube. He paid the boy and asked Sutherland in. The place was empty. He was living in the kitchen, sleeping on a couch next to a little radio. He told Sutherland that he was a very ill man but that the doctors had let him out to settle his affairs. He didn't think he'd live very long, but he had to dispose of his collection of photographs. They all were in packages, on shelves, underneath the worktable in his darkroom. Would Mr. Sutherland mind packing them and sending them to the Library of Congress right away, so he could go back to the hospital? Sutherland was so frightened that Rizzuto would die on the spot that he promised him he'd do it. Then he took him back to the hospital. After that, he visited him three times a week. Rizzuto told him about the photographs; Sutherland asked him if he'd ever heard of Stokes's *Iconography*; Rizzuto said he not only owned reproductions from it but had been trying to do the same thing himself for fifteen years.

The afternoon that Montgomery met Sutherland in the hospital, Sutherland had come thinking he was going to witness Rizzuto's will. When he found out he was named executor, he simply refused. He said he'd done that before for some of his own tenants, but he had no time for it now. He just wouldn't do it. Rizzuto said he was sorely disappointed in him; he had thought of him as his friend. Sutherland said he didn't care what he thought. Rizzuto turned to Montgomery. Would he do it? Montgomery said it wouldn't be advisable since Rizzuto didn't know him. Rizzuto said there was no one else; he'd have to do. So Montgomery agreed. A month later Rizzuto was dead.

When the hospital told him the news, Montgomery called Rizzuto's brother in Omaha. He told him that Rizzuto had died and been cremated. He asked him if he wanted the ashes. Sam Rizzuto said no, he could do anything he liked with them. So Montgomery, who knew Rizzuto had been a veteran, gave them to the army, which buried them on Long Island. Then Montgomery filed the will for probate, sent a copy of the notice to Sam, and, since he had filed many other wills that bore the marks

of family arguments, waited for Sam's lawyer to call with his objections. In the meantime, he said, he took an inventory of Rizzuto's property. Rizzuto's house was a small, three-story brownstone in a very nice neighborhood. Inside, it was poorly kept and full of surprises. On the third floor Montgomery found a dozen suitcases, three steamer trunks, and a footlocker. The footlocker was from the army, but there was far too much luggage, Montgomery thought, for a man who left his house only once a day. On the second floor Montgomery found a darkroom with an enlarger on a long worktable whose shelf was loaded with the packages of photographs that Sutherland later mentioned in his deposition. On the same floor was a studio with shelves of photographic equipment. Montgomery made an inventory: There were two Nikons, a Pentax, a motor drive, a zoom lens, and three telephotos; a four-by-five camera, a two-and-a-quarter, and a panoramic Widelux. There were also a bulk film loader, three tripods, and two pairs of binoculars, one for night vision. Montgomery said he'd wondered about that one. In the basement he found a professionally equipped workshop. There were hand and power tools for every kind of wood and metalwork. There was even an anvil. There were also seven stepladders.

All this time I had been listening quietly. But when Montgomery got to the seven stepladders, I couldn't help myself. Seven ladders? Where had the man climbed, and what had he built? Montgomery smiled and went on with it. On the first floor, he said, he found a room with a desk and, next to it, piles of notes and huge files of correspondence. It appeared Rizzuto had spent a lot of time in libraries. Montgomery found the outline of the book Rizzuto had never completed resting on top of one pile of notes. I interrupted him again. Had he kept it? Did he have a copy? Yes, he thought he did. He excused himself, went into the next room, and returned with a thick file of documents. He handed me three pieces of crumbling yellow paper. On the first page, written in the spidery script of a sick man, were the title and by-line, "Little Old New York, Three Centuries After, by Anthony Angel." On the next was a dedication to his father and mother—"In their adopted country/A cherished New World/They lived with honor/they died with honor"— and on the third, a table of contents. He had intended the first part of his book to have been a chronology, from 1664 to 1964 of "New York, the United States, and the World." The second part was to have been a photographic history, from 1949 to 1964, of lower, mid, and upper Manhattan. Montgomery said that there was a huge mass of correspondence separate from these notes. It looked as if Rizzuto had kept all the letters he'd ever received and carbons of all the letters he'd ever written. The first thing that Montgomery did was to haul the photographs and the files to his office for safekeeping. The photographs filled an empty room. It took him weeks to sift and decipher the files. Years later, after the estate had been settled, and all the photographs shipped to Washington, Montgomery had gone through the files again and retained only those documents he considered essential. All that remained was the thick file he'd carried in from the other room. He opened it and began to read. Occasionally the documents contained things as strange as the stepladders, and I interrupted him.

To begin with, there were documents of birth and education: Born on December 19, 1906. A Sagittarius. Born in Deadwood, in Lawrence County, South Dakota. His father a thirty-year-old named Antonio, a native Italian, described as a contractor. His mother a twenty-nine-year-old named Francesca, maiden name, Scarpino, also Italian, already the mother of two children. Next, an Omaha primary school certificate, this one giving his birthdate not as 1906 but as 1907 and describing his father as a labor agent. Then a graduation certificate from an Omaha technical high school in 1925. And then a set of transcripts from, of all places, a small Lutheran college in Ohio.

Rizzuto had studied the Bible, the life of Christ, and Chinese religion. He had read Shakespeare, Milton, and the American poets; studied biology and bacteriology; learned Greek, French, and, in the summer of 1930, Spanish, at the University of Mexico. He had gotten A's in biology, astronomy, and the life of Christ. Astronomy and the life of Christ? I wondered how much those subjects had to do with a name like Anthony Angel. The only thing certain was that he'd majored in English and minored in history and biology. Two years after he was graduated, he had entered Harvard Law School. In March 1933 he had withdrawn and never returned.

If Montgomery thought anything of the slight coincidence between himself and Rizzuto, he didn't acknowledge it. Instead, he went on with the documents—of income, employment, and military service. There was a draft certificate issued to Rizzuto in New York in 1940. It gave his address as East Thirty-ninth Street, his height as five feet four inches, his weight as 160 pounds, his eyes and hair both as brown. This was followed by a certificate of honorable discharge from the army. It described him as a laborer with blue eyes and an excellent character. A clerk-typist might always have changed the color of his eyes, but I wondered how a well-educated man who had wanted to be a Harvard lawyer had been turned into a laborer? The only answer Montgomery had were a series of payroll slips, the first of them from 1943 and 1944, issued by something called the Red Arrow Bonded Messenger Corporation of Los Angeles. Rizzuto had worked as a messenger? So had Henry Miller. I had thought of Miller when I'd first seen Rizzuto's contacts. And now I remembered the *Tropic of Capricorn*'s Cosmogenic Telegraph Company, that lunatic enterprise whose messengers either vanished as soon as they walked out the door or stuffed their telegrams down the nearest sewer as soon as they spotted an open bar.

In two years of carrying messages for Red Arrow, Rizzuto had earned $1,300— equivalent to perhaps $5,200 in contemporary currency. In 1945 he left the job behind. He moved first to Detroit, Michigan, where he worked for radio station WCAR in the Motor City, then to Providence, Rhode Island, where he worked at a place called the Cherry Web Broadcasting Company. In 1945 Cherry Web had paid him $568; WCAR had paid him a little more; he must have been nothing but a stringer for both of them. A year later he moved again, this time back to New York, where he worked for an operation called Confidential Reports, Inc. I imagined that was when he bought the fancy binoculars. Again, he earned only a little more then $1,000. In three years of carrying messages and selling information, he'd earned less than $3,600—and, I thought, bought a lot of luggage. I asked Montgomery if there was evidence of any other source of income. Montgomery produced letters from several insurance companies; for thirty years Rizzuto had received annuities from policies in the names of his parents. The annuities had been worth only $170 a month, but from 1936 until 1967 they had totaled $63,000. Inflation must have decreased their value, but they might have been enough to feed a single man. I told Montgomery about the hotel room Rizzuto had lived in. The annuities weren't enough to buy a brownstone, or cameras, or fifteen years' worth of film and photo paper. Where had those things come from?

To begin with, Montgomery said, he had found a series of letters to and from patent attorneys and then to and from commercial manufacturing companies. It appeared that Rizzuto had spent years building devices, patenting them, and trying to sell them. He had filed patents for folding platforms, collapsible shelves, retractable coasters, and portable ladders. Every one of them had been without commercial value. But at least the patents explained the workshop, the tools, and the ladders. Sure, I thought, Angelo was trying to get taller. Anthony Angel was trying to get to heaven. But, I asked again, how had he been able to afford the climb?

There were, said Montgomery, an immense number of letters, perhaps 200 in all, that Rizzuto had written after his older brother Frank had died without a will in 1959. Frank had neither a wife nor children, so after taxes, his estate must have been divided in some fashion between his two brothers. During that process Rizzuto had written letters that read as if they'd been thrown over the wall of an asylum. Frank had owned property in both Omaha and Denver, so in each city there were administrators for his estate, attorneys employed by them, and county court judges who presided over the proceedings. By the time Frank's estate had been divided, some of it going to Angelo, but most of it going to Sam, Rizzuto had written letters declaring that everyone connected with the process was insane, or corrupt, or under the influence of an international Jewish Communist conspiracy. He'd probably got the brownstone out of it, but he'd wanted more.

He wrote the Nebraska attorney general, the clerk of the state legislature, and the state insurance director that his brother Frank had been insane and that his brother Sam was so warped, violent, and mutilated a man as to be in need of a legal guardian. He wrote to the Nebraska Bar Association that the attorney retained by the Omaha administrator of Frank's estate was "a vicious Hebrew Shyster" and that his own attorneys, who had failed to defend his interests, were also shysters. He told the Nebraska attorney general that the presiding judge in Omaha was a prostitute. He then wrote letters to sixteen Omaha law firms in search of a new attorney, who, he said, "must be familiar with the tactics of Communists . . . since any lawyer who represents me will be under pressure of Communists, particularly among Jews." He said that his former attorneys had failed to represent him adequately "because of the strong grip that wealthy Jews have over the entire nation—particularly the 'Jew rats' belonging to . . . the B'nai B'rith. . . ".

He wrote similar letters of accusation to the Colorado Bar Association, the Colorado Supreme Court, and the Colorado attorney general, complaining about the administrator of Frank's estate in Denver, as well as about his attorneys and the presiding judge there. Between March and July 1961 Rizzuto wrote sixty-five letters to various members of the Colorado legislature claiming that "the vast majority of Communists in this country are Jews . . . , that Jews . . . 'stick together like burrs,'" and that everyone connected with his brother's estate was a traitor controlled by Communists. He sent copies of these letters to the U.S. attorney general, the IRS, and one U.S. senator and four U.S. congressmen. He then wrote twenty-six letters to the governor of Colorado, in which he charged that the presiding judge in Denver was a psychotic "dominated by Communists." Toward the end of this series of letters he accused the governor himself of cowardice and treachery. He sent copies of all these letters to the President and the U.S. attorney general, to various U.S. senators and congressmen, and to the Colorado Supreme Court, legislature, and attorney general. Perhaps his most astounding letter, said Montgomery, was one to the U.S. attorney general, complaining not about his brother's estate but about the mail: "Your files are filled with my complaints about delays in receiving checks from time to time—delays created by psychotic Communists in the Post Office Department, most of them Jews." Crazy Communist Jews were holding up his annuities.

When Rizzuto died and Sam's lawyers charged him with testamentary incapacity,

Montgomery turned copies of the letters over to them as required by law. Although it seemed from the excerpts Montgomery had read that the man was mad, he was not proved crazy enough for his will to be invalidated. After all, Montgomery had argued, he had never said that Sam was either a Jew or a Communist. In spite of that ruling, I had my doubts about his sanity. Since I'm a Jew, I could neither understand nor forgive his hateful prejudice. Yet, when I first saw his work, I had detected no evidence of his paranoia. I had seen no pictures whose spirit alluded to hook-nosed bankers manipulating the world with their fat, ringed fingers. I had seen dozens of images in his contact sheets of Hasidic Jews, but they were no more or less an exceptional presence than his pictures of sailors or bums. The Hasidim were one of his recurrent motifs, but he photographed them no more often and with an insight neither more nor less intense than nuns and street preachers. Was it possible that one man could be an artist intent on recording the shape and face of an entire world and, at the same time, a man who believed that within that world there was a vast and evil conspiracy against him? Were these multiples of the same person? And if they were, how did they live together? Was the short little man who lived in fear and anger momentarily transformed by the other who lived in art? Did Angelo change into the Angel? Was a creature of rage, fear, and obsession transformed by and into a creature of grace and transcendence? And was the agent of that change the daily act and occasional art of his photography?

There was one more thing I had to do before I could answer these questions or ask myself new ones. I had seen Rizzuto's executor, heard his stories, and listened to his accounts. Before I could return to the place I had begun and look again at Rizzuto's pictures, I had to go to Omaha and talk to what remained of his family. Neither he nor his brothers had had children. The only ones left were his cousins, the children of his father's brother. They had been very young when Rizzuto had argued with his family, never to return. They spoke of him vaguely, as if he had lived long ago, when buffalo covered the Great Plains. One thought he had attended Harvard, Yale, and Cornell and become a lawyer. Another said he had been a successful commercial photographer in New York who had never returned to visit because his business would have suffered without him. Someone else had heard that he had been an FBI agent who worked on special assignment. And there was another who had been told that he had once been President Truman's bodyguard. When I asked about that, she said that a friend of the family had once seen Angelo in a newsreel, dressed in plain clothes, standing next to the President during a ceremony. After a few hours of this I discovered that I knew more about Rizzuto than they did. Since they were linked to him by blood, while I was attached to him only by curiosity, I told them what I knew. In return, since they were kind and generous people who wanted to help if they could, they told me about Rizzuto's father, his brothers, and the world in which they'd lived.

There had never been many Italians in Omaha. Even in 1930 there were only 3,000 of them. In the nineteenth century they passed through as itinerant laborers and wandering musicians. The ones who came in the nineties were peasants from Calabria; the ones who came in the first decade of the next century were Sicilians. Most got off the train with a few dollars in their pockets and headed for the Palazzo Russo, owned by a fruit dealer. Upstairs was a rooming house; downstairs were a restaurant, a saloon, a bakery, a barbershop, a loan company, and a labor agency. All around were warehouses, factories, and railroad spurs. A few blocks away were the brothels. Some got jobs in the smelters and packinghouses. Others found work with contractors. But most worked for the railroads, in the shops, or on construction crews and repair gangs. The railroads controlled large parts of their lives.

In Omaha, on the west bank of the Missouri, were the terminals and junctions of the Burlington, the Illinois Central, the Chicago & Northwestern, and the Missouri Pacific. The city was the terminal headquarters of the Union Pacific, a line originally built by Civil War veterans across 12 million acres of federal land grants, financed by $27 million in government bonds. By 1869, when the tracks of the Union Pacific were linked by a golden spike to those of the Central Pacific near Salt Lake, the venture had cost $94 million. More than half of it had gone to construction companies owned by the railroad's directors, who created a holding company called the Crédit Mobilier, whose stock they used to buy U.S. senators, congressmen, Cabinet officers, a future President, and two Vice Presidents. Within three years those who owned shares of Crédit Mobilier shared profits of between $33 and $50 million. When news of this finally reached the public in 1872, it resulted in the impeachment of two congressmen and a financial panic that brought on a nationwide depression.

The depression of 1873, as well as the one in 1882 and the one after that in 1893, resulted in layoffs and wage reductions which, in the railroad industry, were invariably challenged by workers, who formed unions and went on strike. Whenever possible, the railroads broke these strikes by hiring desperate men from among the most recently arrived group of immigrants. By 1900 the Union Pacific, which was accustomed to buying Cabinet officers, had begun to buy Italian immigrants. During shop strikes in Omaha in 1905 and 1911, it hired Sicilians and Calabrians as scabs. The price these men paid for their jobs was ostracism by the Anglo and Irish workers they replaced. During

the First World War these new men enjoyed good, steady wages, both because rail traffic increased and because the supply of cheap labor from Europe had been cut off. But during the postwar recession of 1921, when wages and hours were cut, the men went on strike. The Union Pacific treated them as it had treated all the others: They were blacklisted and replaced by men as desperate as they had once been.

The blacklisted men found what work they could, either cooking whiskey and selling it to Anglos or doing jobs so menial and ill paid that no one else wanted them. The Sicilians among them deposited their wages and their whiskey profits in a bank owned by a man named Sebastian Salerno. Salerno had begun his career in 1899 first as a shoemaker and then as a seller of secondhand clothing. In 1900 he had got a job as a steamship agent, gone back to Sicily, and begun to export Sicilians to Omaha, where they went to work for the railroads. The men rented rooms in boardinghouses owned by Salerno; they bought food and clothes from his stores, and they took their shoes to his shop to be repaired. Many trusted him to hold their wages or send a portion of them back to their families. By 1908 Salerno had established the Bank of Sicily and begun to make investments. In 1924 a bad real estate deal in Florida carried away the bank's deposits. Salerno moved to California and opened a clothing store. In 1931 a dishwasher who had lost his life savings found Salerno and shot him to death.

An Italian in Omaha seemed to have only two choices, and both were dangerous: Either he let himself be used as a tool by the railroads, or he lived off his compatriots. If the Union Pacific and the Anglos didn't get him, one of his own countrymen might. In 1906 Rizzuto's father, Antonio, took a chance and moved to Omaha. He had been one of eleven children, born in a wretched little village in Calabria, called Rizzuti, a village that was in the very heel of a province that was itself at the very bottom of the Italian boot. Sometime before 1901 Tony and a younger brother, Frank, left for America. There are pictures of them made by photographers in Pennsylvania railroad towns and portraits of them made in studios in Alberta and British Columbia. No one knows how or why they traveled across the continent. The only thing certain is that in 1901 Tony worked as a contractor on an earthen dam being built in Deadwood. From there, with a wife and three children, he went to Omaha and declared himself a labor agent.

To be a labor agent was to be a matchmaker. The only difference was that if the marriage didn't work, the matchmaker might get his legs broken. On one side were the railroads; they always needed temporary help, help that wouldn't strike because it couldn't speak English. On the other were the men who had nothing but their bodies and who always needed jobs; they called a job, any job, their "wealth." The labor agent brought one group together with the other. At the end of the job the company paid the agent; the agent paid himself a percentage, and then he paid the men. It was all a little risky. If the railroad cheated the men, if it said they'd worked only eighteen hours when they'd actually worked twenty, then the agent either had to make up the difference himself or had to start running. Or if on the job the foreman said one thing and the men did something else, then the agent knew that even with a different crew he could kiss the next job good-bye. But if no one cheated anyone else and everyone did as he was told, then one job led to another, and a labor agent often turned into a contractor. He could remain a contractor just as long as he didn't make a promise he couldn't keep or just as long as everyone believed he gave as much as he took. Otherwise, the same thing could happen to him as happened to Salerno, the banker.

Tony got his first jobs as a contractor by doing work no Anglo would touch. He began by cleaning the shit out of cattle cars. By the First World War he was cleaning out troop trains. Soon he was grading roads. By 1925 Rizzuto Brothers Construction was building bridges for the Union Pacific and the Burlington and constructing culverts for the federal government. In nine states, from Iowa to Nevada, the company loaded coal on locomotives and ice on refrigerator cars. The company owned an office building in downtown Omaha, a gravel pit with a gold catcher in Colorado, and a mountaintop in the Ozarks that Tony dreamed of turning into a "labor colony," stocked like a trout pond with immigrants from Calabria. Tony spread his money around: He endowed a football scholarship for Italian students at the state university and published an English-language newspaper in the Italian community. He became a Thirty-second-Degree Mason and did favors for Father Flanagan's Boys Town. He gave lavish parties and invited U.S. senators. He opened a supper club called Dinty Moore's, where men of importance made deals over slabs of prime beef.

By the end of the twenties Rizzuto Brothers had 1,000 men on its payroll. Tony got the contracts and made the investments; Frank ran the operation as his partner. Whenever Frank went out on a job, Tony's son Sam was his driver. One day Sam, armed with a shotgun, came over the hill in a touring car just in time to stop a construction crew from lynching his uncle. When Sam wasn't on the road with Frank, he did things like drive important drunks home from his father's parties. And when he wasn't doing that, he did errands for the Jews who ran some of the rackets in Omaha. He gambled at night and got into fights. He lost an eye when some guy hit him with a bottle. During the day he used to walk around as impeccably dressed as Al Capone.

Tony held the whole operation together until 1934, when he came back from a business trip to Salt Lake and died of a stroke. His three sons and his brother all wanted what he'd left behind. Sam and Frank decided to become the next Rizzuto Brothers. They hired two Jewish lawyers to help them. They needn't have gone to the trouble. Uncle Frank refused to fight; he said he wouldn't walk on his brother's grave. Angelo had just dropped out of Harvard; he was in no shape to do anything. Sam said that "he didn't know his ass from third base." Someone else said that "he got creamed." Angelo's only problem was that he knew more about astronomy than cattle cars. When he realized what his brothers were doing, he warned his uncle and then left town. Once that had been settled, Frank turned the lawyers loose on Sam. Years later one of the attorneys said he'd never seen anything that ruthless.

By 1936 Frank had won control of the business but had destroyed his family. Sam cashed in his inheritance, moved to Miami, and never again spoke to his brother. Frank, in his loneliness, married a blonde who said she was a nurse. A week after the honeymoon she filed for divorce. The newspapers said that not counting the diamonds and the furs, Frank's marriage had cost him $2,500 a day. For weeks he read about what a fool he'd been. Then he went to Denver and had a nervous breakdown. In 1941 Angelo reappeared, trying to sell some mining stock he'd inherited and jointly owned with Frank. Frank didn't want to hear a word. So Angelo went back to his hotel room, laid out some towels, put on a white shirt, and slit his wrists.

It took me three days of listening to learn all this, and another week before I began to understand it, but it took months before I was able to discover what happened to Rizzuto after he tried to kill himself. According to the hospital physician who treated him, Angelo had nearly died from blood loss and shock. When he recovered, he told the doctor that because of his education, his mother and his brothers had cut off his allowance after his father had died, even though he had prostate trouble and needed money for medical expenses. He said that he had tried to kill himself because he thought his brain would explode. He told the doctor that his older brother was crazy but was rich enough to afford his own psychiatrist. The physician listened to all this and then transferred him, at his brother's expense, to a private sanatorium.

He told the admissions staff there that his full name was Angelo Antonio Rizzuto, that he was thirty-five years old, that he lived in Omaha, and that he was a student. He explained that "my present predicament is caused by great ambition; I am trying to fight my way through life alone." He said that while he was riding on a Union Pacific train, traveling to Denver to sell some stock to pay his debts, he began to think about the sinister forces working against him. He described in detail how Frank had deprived him of his inheritance and how his own attorney, a Jew, had betrayed him to work for his brother. He talked of how the two of them were conspiring with powerful businessmen, railroad officials, and Jewish organizations to cheat him, drive him crazy, and murder him. He said that by the time the train arrived in Denver he felt his head would burst. He said he decided to end his own life so he wouldn't become a helpless burden.

Hidden in his story were truths, both real and imagined. To begin with, Angelo had said he was a student. In fact, it had been eight years since he had withdrawn from law school and seven years since the stroke that killed Antonio had deprived Angelo of his father's protection. Now, with too litle knowledge and too little money, Angelo had become a little boy again, fighting a losing battle not only with his older big brother, who was a lawyer, but with his own former attorney. Angelo was frightened not only because his opponents knew more than he did but also because he believed they were allied with all the powerful interests that his own father had somehow managed to tame and bend to his will. Now that his father was dead, there was no one to protect Angelo from either his brother or the world. Frank had stolen his money and his attorney and had betrayed Antonio. Frank may have been the firstborn, but Angelo bore his father's name. It was Angelo Antonio who was his father's true son. His proof was that he would even die like his father: While he was on a business trip to fight for his rights, his brain would swell, burst, and leave him helpless. By imitating his father in death, he would prove that Frank was an evil madman who wanted to dominate him.

It was no coincidence that these thoughts had come to him while he rode on the Union Pacific. Frank had cheated him of his birthright with the help of three Jewish lawyers, two of his own and one he had stolen. Angelo's elaborate generalizations may not have been justified, but his fears were, and his paranoia was something that any Italian who had ever had contact with the Union Pacific in Omaha carried with him like an intestinal parasite. Angelo's father had somehow developed an immunity, but nearly everyone else who worked for the railroad did it at his own risk. It was a company founded on a policy of conspiracy, bribery, and stock manipulation. For thirty years it had used and discarded immigrants like broken hammers. Italians who either worked for the railroad or lived off those who did lived in jeopardy. Omaha was littered with blacklisted men, dead bankers, bootleggers, and one-eyed gamblers. It was a place where fortunes were made from shit and gravel, where uncles were nearly lynched, where women married men for their money, and where brothers robbed brothers. Sam, on his deathbed, said, "It's all blood money." When Angelo went crazy, he told the doctor he needed a rest; the doctor thought he needed insulin shock; what he really needed was another

life in another world. The crazy letters he wrote twenty years later, after Frank had died, were the work of a burn victim who had been caught too close to a mixture of blood and money when it exploded in a confined and desolate place.

When I was young, I had read Dickens, Conrad, and Turgenev and then looked at their faces. The hooded glance of Ivan Turgenev, the sharp eyes of Joseph Conrad, the dreaming gaze of Charles Dickens—their eyes were all the same. And so, I thought, were their souls. I wondered if a profession was nothing but a collective personality, as if it were a hunt that pursued a quarry to whose scent was drawn a particular breed, bred to that chase. Were glassblowers drawn to fire and surgeons to bloody warmth? Why, in the name of God, were there such creatures as photographers? I'd wondered that for years, and now I had one, his private parts spread out in front of me on a table. What I had before me were the remnants of a cripple, an industrial accident, a man with third-degree burns who every day at 2:00 P.M. loaded his cameras and walked. Walked! Walked when he should have been dead. What I had were the remains of a man who had been so deformed and betrayed by his past that he'd hidden himself from the world on which he'd longed to gaze. The old man in T. S. Eliot's poem "Gerontron" had talked of nothing but paradoxes, of vices bred by heroism and virtues forced by crimes. What I had in front of me was a man with no legs who had climbed up on roofs and, standing alone, had recorded the panorama of a whole city struck by the sun. What I had was a pillar saint with a camera.

For months, I had been collecting accounts and chronicles, rumors and suppositions, inventories and lists of documents. Yet no matter how well authenticated the facts, no matter how well articulated the parts, all I had was a body that could neither move nor speak. Then I remembered the old man in the black velvet cap I'd met years ago in the library at Columbia. I'd summoned a ghost then without knowing it. Perhaps I could do it again.

I began by looking, once more, at Rizzuto's contact sheets, slowly at first and then, as my eyes and mind grew accustomed to their cluttered and recurrent detail, more and more quickly. I noted his repetitions again and his methods: 40 pictures of the urn in front of the Public Library; 30 pictures of Christopher Columbus; 250 pictures of the Statue of Liberty. Cityscapes photographed for ten years from rooftops and then from rented small planes and helicopters. Women photographed constantly, either with telephotos or with cameras mounted on tripods, positioned on street corners, their shutters triggered by hand-held cable releases. Somehow, without knowing it, I began to memorize his contact sheets and, in my mind, to splice together their rows of images as if they were lengths of videotape. Instead of reading their frames, one at a time, I began to run whole lengths of them, and as I ran them, I began to hear Rizzuto reciting garbled bits of his life's poetry, as if he were Beckett's Krapp. But unlike Krapp's "spooools," Rizzuto's contacts were composed not of words but of the glances of his eye. Viewed one at a time, his images were neither complex nor ambiguous: Bums looked like bums; sailors like sailors, buildings like buildings, and sorrow like sorrow. By themselves his photographs were without subtle implication. But viewed in lengths, strung together in sequences composed over a period of years, his juxtaposed images formed rhymes, and those rhymes formed patterns with permutations as various as those of a kaleidoscope.

I found a contact sheet Rizzuto made in 1953, on which four frames, each with a single figure, followed one another like the lines of a stanza. In the first, a man walks past a poster of a cancan dancer, mounted on the wall of a building; the effigy kicks up her heels just above his head; he looks up into her petticoats. In the second, Christopher Columbus turns away. He stands alone, on top of a column in midair, as chaste as a saint, his eyes on the farthest horizon. In the third, a man rests on the grass beneath a tree in a park, reclining as gracefully as a picnicker in a Renoir painting. He lies on his side with his back to the hero, the voyeur, and the photographer. In

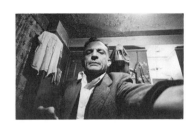 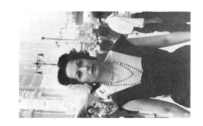 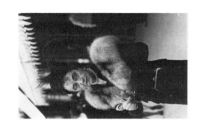

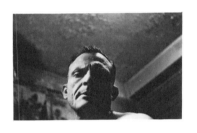 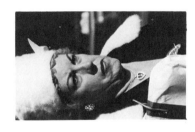 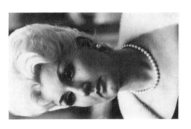

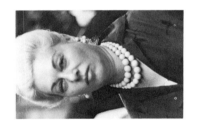 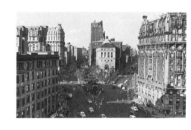 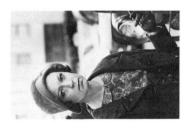

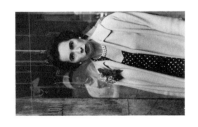 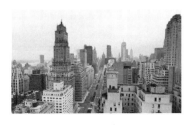 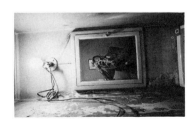

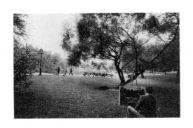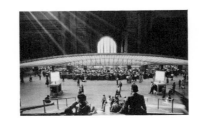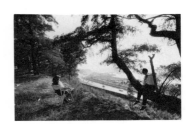
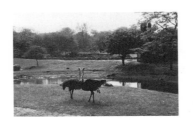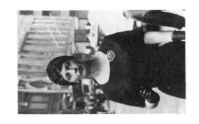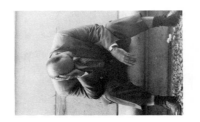
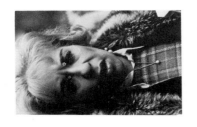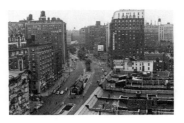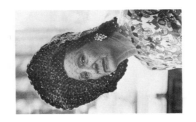
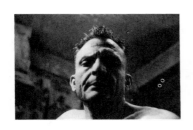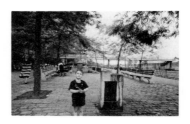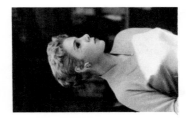

the fourth, a little boy turns and looks back at all the men who have preceded him. He waves to them as he skips across a street. Each image is a replica both of its subject and of the photographer's preoccupation: from sexual arousal to heroic solitude to sylvan isolation to playful innocence.

In another sequence, made in 1959, a beautiful young girl sits alone on a windowsill, painting her nails. In the next frame a middle-aged man rests his belly against a railing and reads his paper, as absorbed in the news as the girl is in her nails. A clock fills the frame next to them. Around its face is written "Time to Repent." Neither the girl nor the man looks up. In another sequence, from 1963, a beautiful woman walks quickly past with her eyes shut as if in grief. The skin of her face is pulled taut, and her dress is pressed against her body as if she were walking into the roaring blast of a furnace. To her right, in the next frame, as large as she is, is a copy of the *National Enquirer.* On its cover are the words "I Cut Out Her Heart and Stomped on It." Next to the word "stomped" is a picture of a young woman, lying on her back with her chest torn open. For fifteen years Rizzuto photographed women whose faces were marked by rage, sorrow, grief, anger, remorse, regret, fatigue, spite, and suspicion. Portraits of those who were either so young as to be marked only by their beauty or so rich and well groomed as to wear cosmetic masks often appear juxtaposed with pictures of nuns or of department store mannequins waiting to be dressed or undressed. Sometimes the women appear trapped in the midst of a sequence whose only other subject is five identical pictures of the wall of a building. Occasionally a woman's picture is juxtaposed with the V-shaped perspective formed by parallel rows of dark buildings bordering an avenue that recedes to infinity. In 1959 Rizzuto made three pictures of women standing beside one of the urns in front of the Forty-second Street Public Library. From the front the urn looks like a gigantic uterus. From the side it appears to be a great stone face bearing an expression of sorrow.

Rizzuto made his first self-portrait in 1953, in December, the month of his birth. During January 1954 he photographed himself twice, at arm's length and eye level, at the end of a series of cityscapes he had made looking up from a street. In August, a year later, in a sequence that begins with pictures of a man resting his head in the lap of a woman, he photographed himself without a shirt, his camera to his eye, reflected in the mirror of his room. A month later, an eye-level self-portrait appears at the end of a series of cityscapes, made from a height, looking across upper Manhattan. Because the point of view of the camera that made the cityscapes is nearly identical to that of the camera that made the self-portrait, Rizzuto appears to be actually viewing the scenes he has previously recorded. During the next nine years this illusion occurs with great frequency: Either the camera angles and eye levels of the self-portraits are identical to those used to record the scenes and cityscapes that have immediately preceded them, or they are reversed, so that a scene photographed from above is immediately followed, in the sequence, by a self-portrait made from below.

For two years Rizzuto stared calmly, then attentively, then anxiously into his lens as if it were a mirror. Sometimes he'd point to it as he pressed the shutter; sometimes he'd furrow his brow. But in December 1955 the face of someone gravely sad appears, staring across at two adjacent frames where a derelict, who has collapsed on the sidewalk, pleads for help from men who only pause to look. Then, at the beginning of 1956, a comedian steps into the frame, wearing Rizzuto's face as if it were a comic mask. As playfully as a drunk and as gaily as a child, he takes picture after picture of his sometimes droll, sometimes delighted, sometimes comically distorted features. His act runs until autumn, when he is replaced by a timid man who bites his lip as he looks across first at a mounted policeman, next at a young man playing his guitar, and then at a little girl standing on the sidewalk. By the spring of 1957 the man has sucked in his lips, hunched his shoulders, hung his head, and lost his shirt. Within a month he is replaced by someone wearing a tragic mask who appears to be carrying a burden far too heavy to bear. From one picture to the next, his pain changes to anger, and his anger into a rage so monstrous that the man himself seems to change into a demon that stares into a pit where, far below, foolish men in costumes march in a military parade while innocent boys play stickball in the street.

In the fall of 1957 Rizzuto reappears; the camera that sank to his belly is now raised nearly level with his eyes, which stare calmly across at a young woman who stands perfectly still in midframe, looking back at him. In December Rizzuto lowers his camera a bit and looks down with resignation at a little boy dragging his dog on a leash. For the next two years he neither raises his camera nor changes his expression as he peers down with stern resignation at a city photographed from above, its avenues streaked with light, filled with crowds, and crossed by grieving and angry women, photographed from a distance.

Sometime in 1959 Frank Rizzuto died, and from January to July 1960 Angelo Rizzuto wrote letters of paranoid accusation but took no pictures of either himself or the city. When he reappears in 1961, he not only has lowered the camera to his waist but has fitted it with a lens with an angle so wide that he seems to be looking down from heaven. The flesh of his face has swollen; his eyes are sometimes hidden by the spectacles of an old man; at times he wears no shirt, but often he wears a coat and tie, and occasionally an overcoat as dark and formal as death. He looks grim, calm, clerical, and indifferent. Behind him,

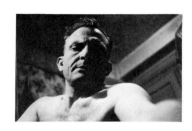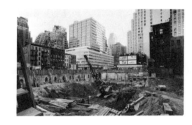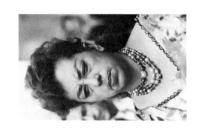

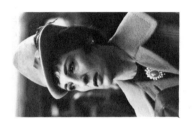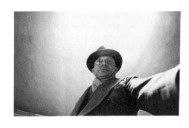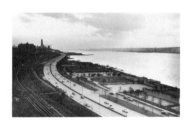

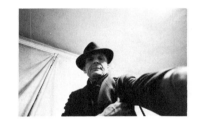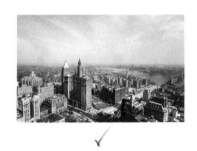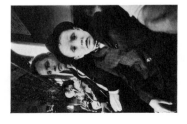

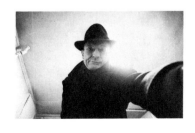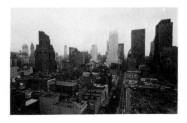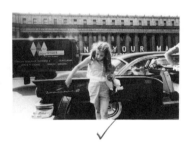

eclipsed by his head, glows a light with no source, like the light of a saint painted by Georges de La Tour. Surrounded by light, he looks down on shoppers and delivery boys, on families huddled on subways, and on vast panoramas of buildings and streets. He has become as remote as a recording angel, bearing witness to a world of pain and geometry.

In a way, he could have been Blume scampering through squares of private meaning, or Prufrock, wandering through certain half-deserted streets, or even Krapp, holding his endless spools of tape up to the light. The pictures he made were acts of homage and appropriation, elements in an iconography of a city permeated by a self. He believed he was recording the physical shape of an outer world when, in fact, he was gathering evidence to serve as a talisman against his own despair. That evidence of a shared mortal predicament he found in the faces of the countless women he photographed. Occasionally he found evidence of hope in the gestures of lovers, the grace of dumb animals, and the games of children. In *A Search for God, in Time and Memory,* John S. Dunne observed a difference between the autobiographies of Rousseau and Goethe and those of Yeats and Sartre. In the eighteenth century, said Dunne, autobiography was an act which affirmed an author's uniqueness in the presence of universal suffering and death, while in the twentieth century autobiography was an effort to discover a shared commonality with the world in order to deny existential loneliness and despair. By photographing himself, Rizzuto affirmed his own presence; by photographing the suffering of others as well as by recording the awesome shape of a man-made world, Rizzuto used his camera to lessen the pain of loneliness and to transcend his fear and anger. He used his camera to confirm himself, to enter and discover the world, and then to rise above it. His loneliness, his persistent vision, and his transcendence are what he shares with the other photographers in this book, all of whom embarked on solitary quests whose success transformed and then restored them to themselves.

Past the Volvo, past the Saab, unlock the door; past the Ducati, chained and balanced on its kickstand, up into shutters made of planks. Past a wall of hubcaps that glint and glimmer like shields and mandalas; the spoked, chromed, and battered bull's-eyes of Mustangs, Starfires, Monarchs, Sevilles, and a Mercedes. Past doors marked "No Admittance," "Ladies," and "Notary"; past a flag, draped and gathered over a door like an opera curtain, into an enormous room without comfort or safety. The air is cold; the light is so dim that anything at arm's length turns into a silhouette. On the wall, thirty yards away, is a police target, its heart torn apart by .22's. A tent has been pitched in one corner, next to some pallets scavenged for firewood. In front of its flap is a motel welcome mat and some smooth stones gathered from a stream bed. Hearts, bolts of lightning, cupids, and a tiger-striped kite hang from the ceiling. Wooden beams, painted white, rise diagonally out of the concrete floor and zigzag like bridge trusses across the space. The walls are covered with objects. The place looks like an apothecary shop stocked with car parts, rubbish, and idols.

Twenty yards from the tent, hanging by a clean rope, resting against a white wall, is the rear door of a black 1948 Hudson, the kind of car that Dean drove in *On the Road.* Its window has been rolled halfway down to let in some air; a pair of high-heeled shoes has been hooked over the glass; an undulating pattern of pucker marks and puncture wounds from rifle bullets moves across the door. Beside it, nailed to a sliding plank door, is a necklace from which hang holy medallions, saints' medals, and votive effigies made of silver. One end of the necklace is nailed to a small poster of Augusto César Sandino, the patron saint of the Nicaraguan revolution. The entire necklace of charms, medals, and medallions stretches across an invitation to Mr. William Burke, photographer, to attend a reception at the American Embassy in Managua. Beneath it is a cracked photograph of a group of armed Sandinistas. Beside them is a small picture of Jesus, lying on his belly, crowned with light. From a distance, he looks as if he has leprosy; up close, the sores turn into a mass of votive effigies.

Nailed to the same wall as the riddled Hudson is a painted tin sign advertising Stull Hybrid Corn. The words "Stull," on the top, and "Hybrid," on the bottom, are embossed in handsome red capitals; in the center is a blue and white cameo portrait of a southern gentleman wearing a coat, bow tie, and broad-brimmed hat. Behind the cameo, crossed like the bones of a pirate flag, are two ears of corn, one yellow, the other blue. The gentleman's eyes, nose, and mouth, the ears of corn, and the words are full of rusted bullet holes that look like the

scars of a pox. Nailed high above all this, in the very center of the wall, are a matching pair of hand-painted mudguards; they bear the words *Todo Pasa* ("Everything passes").

The only sound in the place comes from behind the plank door. It is the voice of a scrubwoman singing softly and sadly in Portuguese about the tender heart of Jesus. She sings a verse, catches her breath, and sings another. Alone, in an old blue velvet chair, Burke sits in his bedroom, nestled by his amplifier, listening to her. His face and his body are those of a man who may have stood too close and too long by the fire. His eyes are brown, steady, and clear; sometimes they glint with humor. His lips are thin; his smile is quick and easy; the flesh close to the bone. The central part of his scalp has lost its hair, and that, along with the lines across his brow and the tuft of beard that grows between his lower lip and his chin, gives him the appearance, at one moment, of a saxophone player and, at another, of a New England farmer who's left the land to hunt whales. He sits staring into the cloudy light that fills his bedroom listening to the sweet, steady voice of the woman. She'd been washing the floor in his rooming house in Recife when he passed by, and she asked him if he'd sinned. It was a question that he'd been asking himself for years. She said she was worried about his soul and then sang him a hymn that sounded like a lullaby. When she finished, he asked her to sing it again so he could record it. Now, in the deep cold of a Boston winter, sitting alone in what had long ago been the warehouse of a brewery and, for the last fifteen years, had been his home, Burke listened and wondered, surrounded by bits and pieces of things that, like the skin of a snake or the words scratched in a cell, alluded to what he was, had been, and would always be.

Behind his chair was a photograph made by the Czech Josef Koudelka; it was a picture of an old man with a hat, a woman in black, and a little girl in white, arrayed in profile around the outer edges of a space empty of everything except the patterns made by the optical convergence of a floor, a ceiling, a wall, and the shadows cast by the figures themselves. For ten years Koudelka had followed the Gypsies of eastern and western Europe. The result was a series of images, stark, stunning, and subtle, whose motives, one curator had observed, were "not psychological but religious."

Hanging in a row beside the picture were a heart, a leg, a slender hand, two human figures, and a breast, all made of wood. They were *votivos,* the offerings by desperate people to Jesus, Mary, or a saint to ward off evil or end misfortune. Looped around the wooden leg was a silver necklace, from which a tiny star, a key, a saber, and two crosses dangled. Years ago, when Burke was awarded a Guggenheim fellowship and set off across the country with his cameras, the inside of his Volvo had been festooned with such charms. A man who'd traveled through Asia and become a Buddhist had given him a tiny buddha with a pointed head from Thailand to add to his collection. The man had laughed, and his eyes had sparkled when he said, "Watch out for him, Bill; he's a trickster." Bill had hung the buddha on a chain next to his other charms and headed west. Six months later, on the way to visit a mountain village recommended by the very man who had given him the trickster, Burke had suffered the worst auto accident of his life. By the time he repaired his car, got rid of the buddha, and made his way back to Boston he learned that the Buddhist had been diagnosed as having bone cancer and was to have his leg amputated above the knee. Burke went to the hospital the night before the operation, and there in the room he met the man's sister. By the time the Buddhist had mastered his crutches, his sister and Burke had fallen in love; a few years later they got married. The wooden leg, draped with charms, hanging from their bedroom wall, was one reminder of what Burke and the woman shared.

Dozens of hats, some with brims, others with visors, hung all over the wall opposite Burke's chair. There were city and country straws, farmer's and fishermen's straws, the wool hat of an Irishman and the gray felts of businessmen, the helmet of a fireman and the coonskin of a hunter. There were Little League and major-league caps; painters' caps, tobacco pickers', truck drivers', and honky-tonk caps. One said

"Coon Ass"; one said "Ruby Lee"; two said "Mack"; and three said "Cat." Tacked to the wall, high above them, looking past and over them, was a poster of a priest named Padre Cicero, who looked like Spencer Tracy, and who'd fought for the poor like St. Francis. When he died, his grave became the goal of pilgrims.

Beneath Padre Cicero was Burke's bed. Across from it was his desk. Just above it were ten rubber stamps. One said, "Good Art"; one had a picture of a pointing hand; another had a fistful of cash; there was one of a star, another of a crowd looking and pointing at the sky, and another of a man riding a motorcycle. There was one stamp with a Colt six-shooter, another of a tortoise, and one of a cock crowing. When Burke had enough work to show, he gave the stamps to his friends and asked them to grade his pictures. As a result, the backs of his best photographs looked like the pages of a well-used passport. Above the stamps was a bulletin board covered with pictures. Next to a postcard of Anwar el Sadat was a picture of a refinisher, wearing an apron and sabots. The picture had been made in the thirties by August Sander, a Munich photographer whose goal of photographing every social type in Germany had been considered decadent by the Nazis, who'd burned his books. Next to the Sander was a postcard of a Cadillac smashing into a pyramid of burning TV's; next to that was one of an office chair on fire in a conference room. Beneath it was a $10 bill that had been torn in half and burned at the edges. Near it, pinned next to each other, were two cloth patches, the kind worn by mechanics and repairmen. One said "Bill"; the other "Ralph." Ralph had been a black dog who was Bill's only companion when he traveled through Kentucky, taking pictures of every sweet and sad human being he met. Bill would stop in a strange place to take a picture, and Ralph would jump out of the car. Bill would rush after him, camera in hand, while Ralph would piss on someone's mailbox, or get too familiar with a German shepherd, or simply disappear under a porch. By the time Bill had found him and saved his skin or apologized for his lack of breeding, the people whom he wanted to photograph considered Burke harmless enough to take their picture; Ralph knew exactly what he was doing, and so did Bill.

There were two pictures on the bulletin board of Burke and the woman whose brother had lost his leg. There was also a picture of the woman who'd been Burke's companion for five years before that, dressed like a drum majorette, high-kicking in front of a school marching band. The girl had been the child of a diamond cutter who, in his middle age, had developed a passion for cleanliness, which he satisfied by collecting vacuum cleaners of every size, shape, and capacity. In his kitchen were several hand vacuums for crumbs and cuttings; in the garage was a four-wheel monster that could suck up the dirt of a municipal auditorium; in the basement was a machine that could clean out a bilge; and in the upstairs and downstairs closets were lengths of hose, racks of chrome extenders, and dozens of snouts, nozzles, and heads that could beat and sweep at the same time. The man's child grew into a young woman fascinated by surgery, scars, and mutilation. She became an artist who made portraits of herself draped with chicken skin, in which she had made stitches and to which she attached jeweled pins, earrings, and hemostats. When she herself entered the hospital for minor surgery, she had had color pictures made of the procedure and had then cut and arranged the images of her own flesh in kaleidoscopic, crystalline shapes. Soon she became interested in oral surgery and decorated the bathroom in Burke's loft with false teeth, bite blocks, chrome syringes, toothbrushes of every color, dental forceps, probes, retractors, and straight razors. Her favorite book was a work called *Crash* written by a man who had survived a head-on collision. He wrote of the erotic quality of the instruments and uniforms of his nurses and of the perversely sexual nature of the restraints which bound him while he was in traction. The part of the book she'd liked most was the author's description of marks left on his body by the steering wheel and the dashboard.

Burke found neither her art nor her interests bizarre. He had always been attracted by extremes and, as a photographer, had long ago come to believe that appearances were marks left by collisions between the world and human character. One of his favorite passages was from an introduction written by James Agee to *Many Are Called,* a book of portraits of subway riders made by Walker Evans. Agee spoke of each rider as "an individual existence as matchless as a thumbprint or a snowflake. Each wears garments which . . . are exquisitely subtle uniforms and badges of their being. And each carries in the postures of his body, in his hands, in his face, in his eyes, the signatures of a time and place in the world. . . . [T]he simplest and the strongest of these beings has been so designed upon by his own existence that he has a wound and a nakedness to conceal, and guards and disguises by which he conceals it." As a photographer Burke spent his time looking for those existential wounds.

His own grandfather had been a surgeon who, for fifty years, had cut and healed the bodies of half the population of an industrial river valley. Every Sunday, when Burke was a boy, he and his family had eaten dinner at his grandfather's, and as the old man carved the turkey, they would listen to him talk of the surgeries he had performed. A day before the old man unexpectedly died, Burke had begun to read a copy of *Mortal Lessons* by the surgeon Richard Selzer. On the way to his grandfather's funeral, Burke had read that "man is albuminoid, proteinaceous. . . . Woman is yolky, ovoid. . . . Both are exuberant bloody growths. I would use the defects and deformities of each . . . for I know that it is the marred and scarred and the faulty that are subject to grace. . . . It is the exact location of the soul that I am after. The smell of it is in my nostrils. I have caught glimpses of it in the body diseased. If only I could tell it. Is there no mathematical equation. . . ? So much pain and pus equals so much truth?" Every Sunday, as the child of an Italian mother and an Irish father, Burke had gone to church, absorbed the rituals of the blood and body of Christ, and then had gone to dinner and listened to his grandfather's endless table talk of surgery. If Agee talked of wounds, Selzer of the marred and scarred, and the diamond cutter's daughter of collision and mutilation, who was Burke to doubt there was a relationship between outer state and inner grace?

Burke clicked off the tape player. He'd heard and remembered enough. He crossed the bedroom, slid open the door, and headed for the refrigerator for a beer. The only trouble with living the way he did was that it wasn't easy to forget. When he looked one way, there on the kitchen wall was a bas-relief of the Devil tempting Christ. When he turned the other, there in the middle of the floor, the only source of heat other than the stone-cold radiators, was a wood-burning stove made of a fifty-gallon oil drum that he'd bought during his two years of wanderings through Kentucky. There were six more hands, cut off below the elbow, resting on top of the bookcase. Hanging above them on the wall, ten feet apart, were two pictures that appeared to balance each other like weights on the beam of a scale. To the right was a photograph that Robert Frank had made while riding on the roof of a bus, traveling across a high plateau in Peru in 1948. In the foreground of the picture were the hats and backs of the other passengers. Before them stretched a road that vanished in the distance, empty of everything but a rider on a donkey. Beyond them were an infinite plain, a butte, and a sky of clouds. On the wall to the left of the Robert Frank photograph was a picture Burke had made of a fat man, his daughter, and his new baby. The man had been smoking Winstons and drinking beer in complete silence in a bar in the middle of the week in West Virginia. The skin underneath his eyes looked as if it had been broken with a harrow. He'd wrapped one arm around his daughter as if she weren't thirteen but his girl friend. He'd cradled his new baby in the crook of his arm. The child lay on its back, its head big and pale, its mouth and eyes open, looking as if it had just died. The man and his children had looked so marked by something so deadly but, in Burke's experience, so obscure that when he'd looked up from his beer and noticed them, he'd been frightened. He'd walked up to them, made some dumb excuse about wanting to photograph the baby, and then he'd just fired away, making exposure after exposure, sweating

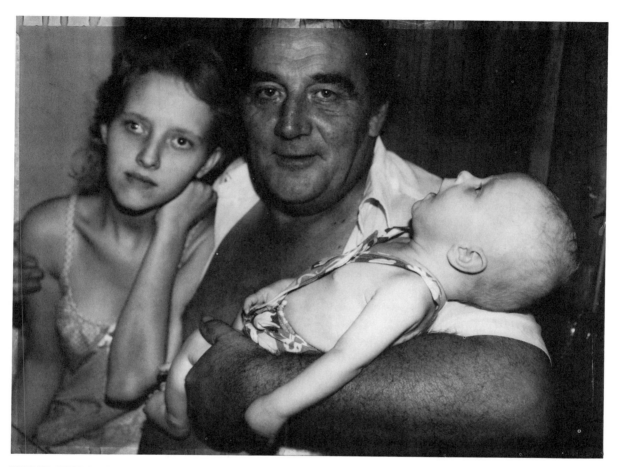

KERMIT, WEST VIRGINIA, 1979

through his shirt. He'd had a kind of Polaroid film in the camera that produced a print for the subject and a negative for the photographer. He kept piling the prints on the bar in front of the man, saying, "How about another?" and "How about another?" The man just looked at him, while the girl's skin glowed in the light of the strobe.

Burke spun around and headed back to the refrigerator for another beer. There was a hand, holding a dog biscuit, nailed through its palm to the wall behind the refrigerator. Hanging beside it was a revolver that would have looked more convincing if it hadn't have been made of bright blue plastic. Above the gun and the crucified hand was a little plastic bag that looked as if it had in it the freeze-dried contents of a drunk's stomach. Just below all this was a wooden rack that held kitchen knives. Whenever Burke sat in the chair in his bedroom with the door open and looked across to the far, opposite wall, the rack appeared near the center of his field of vision. There were five knives, points down, stuck through slits in the rack. Below them was a glass-enclosed frame that in a more conventional kitchen might have displayed an illustrated recipe for *boeuf bourguignon*. Whatever had been there, Burke had replaced with a chromolithograph of a naked, blue-eyed, brown-haired St. Catherine Tekakwitha, standing in chains in a prison cell, enveloped by undulating flames. In the lower-left-hand corner of the print were the words *anima sola* ("soul alone"). The flames in the print burned upward; the knives in the rack pointed down; the lonely soul reached toward heaven.

Thirty years ago, in an essay entitled "Aion: Researches into the Phenomenology of the Self," in *The Secret of the Golden Flower*, Carl Jung had written of the anima ("my Lady Soul") as the archetypal feminine element of a man's unconscious, as that part of his psyche that, once made conscious, imbued him with fecund warmth, emotion, and intuition and that, inevitably projected onto a woman, accounted for his falling in love with her. The anima displayed on Burke's wall was a soul in distress, just as one of the women he had known and loved had been a woman of sorrow, met on the eve of amputation, and the other had been a woman in torment, obsessed by loss and mutilation. The women he'd loved and the *anima sola*, trapped behind glass in a rack in his kitchen, were, in fact, projections of his own soul in jeopardy. It was this soul that not only covered the walls of his loft with symbols of doubt, loss, anguish, innocence, longing, and escape but placed him, camera in hand, at the intersection of events whose participants appeared to have souls in as much need of salvation as his own. In search of solace, Burke was like a starving man walking down a street who often found the quarter he was after. His own spiritual preoccupations, combined with an alertness to the language of things and the meaning of appearances, often placed him at the still point of a world which circled him as if its inhabitants were characters caught in the coincidences of an eighteenth-century novel. In the essay "The Structure and Dynamics of the Psyche," Jung called such coincidences synchronous or acausal connections and defined them as "the simultaneous occurrence of a certain psychic state with one or more external events which appear as meaningful parallels to [it]." Jung quotes Albertus Magnus, the fifteenth-century alchemist, saint, and philosopher who spoke "of a certain power to alter things [which] indwells in the human soul and [which] subordinates other things to her, particularly when she is swept into a great excess of love, hate, or the like." The excess that often swept Burke's soul was one of sorrow and hope against hope; combined, the two emotions often attracted elements of the world as if the object Burke carried were not a camera but a lodestone.

Burke and I had first met in Louisville, a river town which is literally and figuratively halfway between Pittsburgh and New Orleans. It is a place where people and things can be made to appear and disappear; where the principal legal industries are kitchen appliances, bourbon, cigarettes, and horse racing; where various fried foods are first conceived and test-marketed before they are revealed to the American people; and where the characteristic sound of a winter's night is that of empty beer cans blowing down the street. Whether because of its present climate or because the region was once covered by an inland sea, it is a place of time warps and temporal vortices, where the present filters as slowly as sunlight into the depths of the ocean and where the inhabitants of whole neighborhoods restlessly circle the sunken shapes of ideas, social conventions, and artifacts characteristic of such years as 1927, 1941, and 1963. It is a city where shops that sell cards and magazines are listed as bookstores, where stables are cleansed and turned into fashionable restaurants that serve spinach salad dressed with hot bacon fat, and where the population is so homogeneous that in the financial district, at noon, the only way to tell the difference between a bum and a bank president standing side by side, waiting for the light to change, is by their clothes and the relative alcohol content of their blood.

Burke had come there in 1975 at the invitation of an acquaintance of his, a photographer named Ted Wathen, whose family had made a fortune designing and manufacturing commodes for every public rest room in the United States. Wathan was so tall, handsome, and good-natured that dogs, horses, and children were immediately attracted to him, while adults quickly came to like him as soon as they discovered that someone so much bigger than they meant them no harm. Whether because of the man's charming presence or because of the patriotism and patronage unleashed by the Bicentennial, or because federal arts administrators and panelists had read and believed *On the Road, The Grapes of Wrath,* and *The Electric Kool-Aid Acid Test,* three state and federal agencies had given Wathen enough money to conduct a two-year photographic survey of the state of Kentucky. Wathen had invited Burke and another photographer named Bob Hower—a fellow so open-faced and good-looking that few people noticed the ring in his ear—to join him on the project. The three of them had drawn lots and divided the state's counties among them, and for the next two years, with only their dogs for companions, they'd traveled everywhere, taking pictures of everything that moved and many things that didn't. Eventually I met them, saw their work, and was amazed.

Six years later, with only one eye working, I arrived in Boston to talk to Burke. Two days before I'd left my home in Atlanta to visit him, I'd accidentally scratched the cornea, and by the time Burke met me at the airport I felt as if sharp little pieces of metal were caught under my eyelid. Nothing like that had ever happened to me before. I had come a great distance to talk to Burke and look at his work, but I discovered I could neither see out of one eye nor concentrate because of the pain. Burke just smiled and told me that long before, he'd made an appointment for the following day to photograph eye surgery at a clinic. I had heard about Burke's luck, but that was the first time I'd been absorbed by it. The next morning Burke took me with him, introduced me to a specialist, who patched my eye and relieved me of my pain, and then left me to watch color videotapes of cornea transplants while Burke went to take his own pictures of operations in progress. That afternoon Burke stood me on his roof and photographed me squinting and shivering in the sun. The print he eventually made revealed me to be as painfully marked as any of the other people he'd met on his journeys.

I told Burke that I had $50 in my pocket to buy us a good dinner or anything else we wanted. Since it was so cold, I proposed that instead of food, we buy some firewood. Burke wasn't so sure. He suggested that in honor of Kentucky, whose native bourbons were as various as the wines of France, we should buy some whiskey. We compromised. Burke made do with a few cases of Canadian ale and some Makers Mark; I rested my feet against the stove he'd bought in Kentucky and while Burke sipped and paced, and while I tried to stay warm, he told me the story of his life.

He said he remembered a nap during a summer day. Birds were singing; a beautiful, soft green light filled the room. He had been lying asleep in his crib when he felt a shadow pass over him. He woke up in complete horror. It had been nearly forty years since it happened. Whenever he went home, he went up to his old room, and, every time he looked, it was filled with the same soft green light he remembered.

Every time he found it beautiful. And every time he wondered where the shadow and the horror had come from.

He had lived with his parents and his older sister in a house on the shore in New England. He had been born in 1943, in the spring, in the sign of Aries, a sign of fire and iron, the symbol of which is the lowered head of a charging ram. His mother was the child of a self-made man who had become a surgeon because he was good with his hands. Her father had sent her to college during the Depression; when she was graduated, she lived at home and taught typing and shorthand. Bill's father was the son of a sweet and tender Irishman who served a family as gardener, groom, and chauffeur. Bill's father had gone to college on an athletic scholarship. He'd played baseball and basketball and then become a cookie salesman, stocking the shelves of stores with vanilla wafers, Oreos, and honey grahams. One day he was making a sale in a drugstore when he noticed a girl at the counter. When he returned on his route a few weeks later, she noticed him. They talked. It was the middle of the Depression. They both had jobs; they'd both been to college; they both were lonely. He was ten years older than she was. They talked some more and then got married. She moved out of her father's house into a bungalow. He kept selling cookies. They felt safe. Three years later she bore a girl; three years after that she bore Bill. They moved out of the bungalow into her father's

summer house. He'd given it to them after the second child. In return for that and many other things, she obeyed her father until he died.

Her father, Bill's grandfather, had been the cherished only son of a large family ruled by a tyrannical little man so frugal that he insisted his children save for toilet paper the printed wrappers of the pears, plums, and oranges he sold from his stand. When the boy grew to be a young man, he resolved to become a doctor, against the advice of his schoolteachers who doubted that the university would admit the child of parents born in Naples. What his teachers didn't know was that he'd always had his way. He became the first Italian admitted by the university from his town. He lived at home and studied into the night. He knew he didn't have the polished manner that would make him a rich general practitioner, but he had hands so finely shaped, with fingers so quick, supple, and strong, that they could have belonged only to a man born to be a surgeon. They were like beautiful little animals growing from his wrists, covered with white, translucent skin, from which grew tiny black hairs. While he talked, he kept them in his pockets, where they practiced tying and untying surgical knots inside empty matchboxes. After his residencies he opened a general surgical practice. He traveled through the nearby mill towns of the river valley, first in a buggy or a sleigh, depending on the season, then in Packards, and finally in Cadillacs. He did tonsillectomies on kitchen tables, he performed appendectomies in bedrooms, and he delivered babies, when he had to, on sterile rubber sheets he carried in his bag. The mills were full of gears, belts, pulleys, and lifts that crushed, tore, and broke the limbs of their workers. If anything was left, he set it; if little remained, he amputated. He charged his patients according to their incomes. If they had no cash, then they paid in kind: if not in turkeys, then in wine; if not in wine, then in fruit; if not in fruit, then in the care of his house and his grounds. Wherever he went, there were people obliged to him.

He insisted on treating his daughter's children. His care was expert, and it was free, but its price grew year after year. One Sunday, when Bill was seven, his mother dressed him for church but then packed his little bag. Bill tried to ignore it, he wasn't going on a trip. Then his parents put him in the car and drove him to the hospital. His grandfather was waiting. The halls smelled of ether and disinfectant. His grandfather was going to operate on him. Bill had watched him carve the meat of many roasts. He was going to cut him open; his mother hadn't warned him; there was no one to protect him. When he woke up, they told him he'd had a hernia operation.

Whenever anything went wrong, Bill fell into his grandfather's hands. And every Sunday, no matter what, the whole family ate with him. There was no escape. Sometimes it was baked ham and sweet potatoes followed by big needles of gamma globulin; sometimes it was spaghetti and meatballs followed by diphtheria shots. The old man would sit at the head of the table, making his cuts and slices, talking about the time he'd inserted a sliver of rabbit bone into the broken halves of a man's thigh or explaining, as if he were a cabinetmaker, how he'd repaired a man's knee that had been bent nearly backward. After dessert he'd show the pictures. No one would say anything. Then the old man would grin and ask Bill, "Where do you hurt?" but before Bill could deny it, his grandfather would repeat the question in German, then in French, then Polish, then Italian. Bill would keep his head down, listening for the sound of any syringes boiling on the stove in the kitchen, sniffing the air for steam.

When Bill thought of his grandfather, he thought of pain with no protection. He'd learned his right hand from his left after his grandfather had sewn up his palm without anesthetic and left a scar. Once, when he'd torn his fingernail, the old man had pulled off what was left and then jeered at him. "What's wrong with you?" he'd asked. "It doesn't hurt! It doesn't hurt *me!*" he'd said. Bill grew afraid of him. If Bill's parents knew, they never talked of it. They talked of very little. They lived in the house the old man had given them and they brought him their children. Bill's father traveled; Bill's mother stayed home and obeyed her father. By the time Bill was twelve, his grandfather had taken out his tonsils, sewn up his hand and his face, torn out his fingernail, stuck a dozen needles in him, and operated on him twice for hernias. Bill used to climb the stairs in his house and look up at the crucifix on the wall. He wondered why he didn't look like Jesus. He already had almost as many scars.

At Sunday school the only lessons that interested him were the stories of martyrs, especially the stories of children who had denied temptation, been killed by accident, and then gone to heaven. When he was twelve, he'd seen a truck run over his dog. Every night he'd prayed for Piper's soul. One Sunday he asked the nun if dogs went to heaven. The nun grew angry, but he asked again. He'd loved Piper and wanted to know when he'd see him again. The nun snapped at him, "Dogs don't have souls." Her answer changed him completely. He decided that if heaven didn't have dogs, it was no place for him. At confirmation he took the name of St. Francis and declared himself to be a soldier of God. He didn't believe a word of it. The only thing he knew for certain was his own guilt. Every month he went to confession and was forgiven for whatever it was that filled him with dread. Every night he said his prayers. For seven years, until he was in high school, he asked

God for favors. He prayed for his dog, and sometimes he prayed for his father.

At night, after dinner, when he was home, Bill's father would sit and read the paper. Bill would come up behind him, slide his hands down between the cushion and his back, and smell his hair and clothes. His father wouldn't say anything. He was an athlete who always played to win. For as long as Bill could remember, he'd been the tennis champion of his neighborhood. Bill's older sister had played softball and basketball, but when Bill went out for Little League, he couldn't catch a thing. His father had been watching; he hadn't said a word, but Bill knew. A year later a young man beat his father in the tennis tournament. Bill wept and was frightened. His father was growing old. Bill asked God to take care of him.

When Bill was thirteen, he looked as bright and handsome as a kid on the front of a cornflakes box. He ran across the dunes and played in the woods near his house with friends. Everyone had a .22 rifle, but nobody got hurt. In the sixth grade, the same year his dog died and his grandfather took out his tonsils, he won a scholarship to a private school and left his friends behind. The school was one of the most exclusive in the area; for some reason its trustees had decided to open it a crack to the outside world. The scholarship had been publicly advertised; hundreds of boys had competed for its prize. Bill had never expected to win it; his triumph was as remarkable as his grandfather's admission to medical school. The success nearly killed him.

Every morning at six-thirty, he woke up and was driven for forty minutes to a school attended by the sons of rich Anglo-Saxons and wealthy Jews—boys who were as much the same as and as well acquainted with each other as Bill had been with the friends he no longer saw. He was supposed to be a perfect athlete, but the only thing he liked about football was the helmet. In the winter, in the afternoons, he practiced in a pool that smelled of chlorine and the vomit of anyone who had had too many helpings at lunch. At meets, he swam the 200-yard freestyle, always finishing two lengths behind the star who'd beaten him, always ending the race alone, listening to the stands cheer the winner, always pulling himself up out of an empty pool while the crowd watched him in silence and the guys in the next medley nervously shook themselves out behind their diving blocks. Mornings were never good for him. He'd walk into class glassy-eyed and unprepared, straight into the merciless questions of masters who expected him to live up to his title as the school's Morgan Scholar. After lunch was often worse, since it was then that the 200 students of the first, second, and third forms took turns giving speeches to each other in junior assembly. Bill would stand behind the curtains of the stage, waiting his turn, gulping air, trying to keep his lunch down, terrified of walking across to the lectern and stammering out a speech based on some story he'd cribbed from *Reader's Digest.*

He went to the school for five years, each year doing a little worse than before. Somewhere in the middle of the stammers, the last places, the forty-minute drives, the loneliness, and the makeup exams, he began to draw cars and motorcycles on the blackboards. Every empty classroom had a chalk sketch of a Ferrari or a Ducati in it. He daydreamed of motorcycles whose precision, power, and control joined with his body, amplified his slightest movement, and sent him, roaring, across space. His headmaster watched him carefully. One Halloween Bill had been cutting clotheslines in his own neighborhood when he missed and sliced open his scalp. The next day, when he came to school, stitched and patched, the headmaster asked him what had happened. When Bill told him, the man decided that the Morgan Scholar was fast turning into a hood. He was certain of it when, in the spring, Bill broke all the rules and roared into the parking lot on the back of a road racer. At the beginning of the eleventh grade, the school's executive committee sent a letter to his parents expressing its regrets that it would be unable either to renew his scholarship or to recommend him for college placement.

Bill found a place for two years at a boarding school and then got into a small private college full of smart but predictable young men who'd almost made it into Dartmouth and bright but conventional young women who hadn't gotten into Wellesley. His tuition was paid by his grandfather, who gave him a long lecture about becoming a professional. Bill's tests showed he had an aptitude for architecture and city planning. He decided to study art history. Most of his time he spent skiing and repairing motorcycles. He took a painting course from a man who'd studied at the Rhode Island School of Design. "You like this?" his teacher had asked. "You can do this. It's a way to live."

The summer before his junior year he went to Cuba as part of a construction crew employed by an American firm building a plant to produce drinking water for the naval base at Guantánamo. For eight weeks he worked in the dust and the heat behind the guarded perimeter of the base. There were no women. There was nothing to do but work and stare out to sea. He spent his time reading *The Plague* by Albert Camus. Within a few weeks he felt as if he were reading about his own predicament. *The Plague* is a book whose ostensible subject is an outbreak of bubonic plague in the port city of Oran, in French colonial Algeria. Its pages are littered with putrescent corpses of rats, men, and children who have died painfully. It is a chronicle of the effects of epidemic death and suffering on those who can flee neither the sight nor the risk of disease because of a quarantine. The wise and the foolish, the innocent and the guilty, young and old, prey and predator, lover and beloved either die in agony or survive for no reason. At the beginning of the book a writer of independent means, a man named Tarrou, sits on his balcony, apparently so disengaged that he seems to observe "events and people through the wrong end of the telescope." In the course of the book he reveals an unconventional moral code, one not of kindness but of comprehension. He declares that it is blind moral ignorance of human suffering that breeds murder, whether legal or illegal, as surely as microbes cause disease. The entire human race, he says, is dying of advertent and inadvertent homicidal violence, as surely as the citizens of Oran are dying of the plague. Just as those who treat the sick and bury the dead of the city cleanse and inoculate themselves to prevent their own and others' deaths, so, he insists, must men remain morally alert and clear-sighted to save themselves and others from killing off the human race for the best of reasons. As for himself, he confesses that long ago he decided to support whoever were the world's victims, whether they were outcasts or criminals, in order to prevent doing any more damage. "The good man, the man who infects hardly anyone, has the fewest lapses of attention."

Burke was only twenty years old, but he understood Tarrou. He had already suffered enough at the hands of others who'd caused him pain while they spoke of doing him good. His grandfather had tortured him with his cures and treatments; his private school scholarship had been a success that made him feel like a failure. Sometime before he finished *The Plague*, Burke went to the base's post exchange and bought a 35 mm camera. Tarrou had spoken of clear-sightedness and comprehension as if they were moral qualities. One of the first pictures Burke took was of a man, silhouetted against the sky, reaching out to another man, passing him a hose. Burke had studied enough art history to recognize the gesture of Michelangelo's spark of life. He knew what he was doing: "It was a religious reference, brought up by what was in front of me."

He went back to college and learned how to print his negatives in a rathole of a dark-room under a dormitory. One of his friends had been to Mexico and returned with a bag of peyote. Burke ate a few pieces of cactus and watched the world break into proto-types. Everyting became a perfect symbol of itself. His girl friend became Woman; his friend became Friend. He looked at his hand and it turned into a claw, covered with scales. He flexed it and felt the hook. He looked away and it stopped. Then he looked again. This time his fingers had become the claws of a lizard. He watched the scales travel up his arm. He was frightened and looked away again, but the scales didn't stop. He was turning into a creature with a beak, its body a symbol of sin and the physical world. If his mind remained inside it, he would die. He flexed his fingers, and he was free.

A week later he ate more cactus and took a walk. The love he felt for the strangeness of the world poured over him in a wave. He watched a crowd of students follow each other along a sidewalk. They didn't realize that they could step off the walk, that it was only a convention of concrete laid over the earth itself. He made his way to a hill near a grove of trees and lay down on the slope. He felt his back disappear into the ground. He looked out and across at the dark woods, the treetops nearly level with his eyes. He blinked, and a flight of black-birds wheeled out of the woods like a school of fish twisting through coral. The birds swerved back into the dark woods, then emerged again, banked, and then dived from their height into the trees. Again and again the formation emerged and disap-peared into the grove, a swarm of living creatures, a single but variable whole, dis-appearing and reappearing out of a grow-ing mass of living things. Dark into dark, flight into grove, birds into trees, men into the ground and out again, forever. Burke knew then that there were no distinctions, that objects were animate, that death was only a dispersal, and life a reformation. After years of feeling guilty and being for-given, he'd had a revelation of God in na-ture that had nothing to do with sin and absolution.

That summer he went to England and bought a Norton motorcycle; then he crossed the Channel, drove east across the Continent and headed south, on dirt roads, past oxcarts and men in pointed shoes, through Yugoslavia, into Greece. In Athens he met two college friends, and together they crossed into Italy, drove through Provence, and then traveled across the peninsula. In the early mornings they cruised through the yellow dust of the high plateaus; at noon they found shade and inspected their cycles; at night they drank wine, looked at the stars, and slept in stables beside their machines. The loneliness of their travel through a strange country made them feel vulnerable; that vulnerability bred fear but also alertness, and that alertness dilated their pupils and filled their lungs with oxygen. They became strangers who saw everything, drifters along an edge between things simple and strange. By the time they crossed into North Africa, Burke had become a man who paid attention. He returned to America and noticed that his mother had never left her father and that his own father kept to his route. He resolved to become a photographer and to travel so that he could see.

When he was graduated from college, he applied to the Rhode Island School of Design. He'd heard of a master photographer there named Harry Callahan. The school accepted him not as a graduate but as an undergraduate since he had had no formal training in art. After three years of instruction he entered the school's graduate program. Whatever he knew about photography, he had learned from his own experience and from the few books then devoted to photographs as either art forms or documents. He knew the work of Atget, the tireless chronicler of the streets, squares, buildings, and gardens of *fin de siècle* Paris. He knew *The Family of Man*, a book of photographs derived from an exhibition curated, in the early fifties, by Edward Steichen of the Museum of Modern Art, a book which celebrated the common hopes, fears, joys, and sorrows of humanity and which used photographic sequences to advocate racial and political equality, justice, compassion, prayer, and world peace. Burke also knew the work of Eugene Smith, a *Life* photojournalist who had recorded the sorrow and terror of the Pacific war, the round of life and death in a Spanish village, the work of white country doctors and black midwives, and the faces and gestures of such culture heroes as Albert Schweitzer and Charlie Chaplin. Burke had also seen, in reproduction, the precise, sensual still lives and nudes of Edward Weston and the transcendental, psychologically evocative images of Minor White. The summer before he began graduate school, he read *Let Us Not Praise Famous Men* while working on a fishing boat off the Atlantic coast. The boat would set out from New Bedford and head for the Georges Bank; hours would pass before a school of tuna or mackerel was spotted. In the meantime, Burke would lie on a bunk, rocking in the swell of James Agee's lyrical prose.

All summer he read of the faces, bodies, clothes, houses, and tools of poor white Alabama tenant farmers described as if they were heroes and heroines in a frieze by Phidias and Praxiteles. All summer he stared at the photographs Walker Evans had made of the same people, their houses and possessions, succinct photographs whose subjects, whether animate or inanimate, appeared to be beautiful but damaged objects.

Because of everything he had read and seen, Burke came to believe that photography was a morally redemptive art form which could depict the world transfigured by the Good, the Beautiful, and the Sublime. Because of what he had experienced, he came to think of the camera, like peyote, as a tool that could be used to discover the subliminal order and unity of all things. He listened carefully when Harry Callahan, his teacher, who usually spoke with the understated reticence of a shoe salesman, declared that to spend a life in photography was an undertaking equivalent to the building and painting of the Sistine Chapel. Each time Burke showed him his work, Callahan said nothing about his composition or print quality but rather asked him about his motives. "What do you care about?" he'd ask. Again and again: "What do you care about?"

One day Frederick Sommer, another master photographer, came to the school as a guest lecturer. Sommer told how he had once noticed that the musical scores of the great nineteenth-century composers had a remarkable visual integrity. As an experiment, he said, he had written several scores based not on harmonic or melodic conventions, of which he was ignorant, but on those of graphic design. He claimed that when his pieces were performed by musicians, the audience experienced them as coherent musical compositions. He concluded, as a result, that the auditory structures of music and the visual ones of graphic design and photography shared laws of composition, and that visual appearances were one of the key elements for understanding and replicating the universe. Sommer then showed his own photographs. There was one of an amputated foot; another of a series of chicken heads, arranged in rows; and a third of the desiccated corpse of a coyote. Burke became confused and raised his hand. "What about BEAU—TY?" he asked. Sommer answered that beauty was an insufficient criterion for the making of art. Burke left the lecture wondering if the Good, the True, and the Beautiful were as relevant to his work as he had imagined.

That summer he saw an exhibition entitled "Just Before the War" and began to have serious doubts about the photographic importance of the Sublime. The photographs he saw had been made during the Depression by staff members of the Farm Security Administration, a division of the Department of Agriculture. The FSA's mandate had been to record the impact of the Depression and the effect of the domestic policies of the Roosevelt administration on the American people, particularly on those citizens who had lived as farmers and workers on the land. The FSA's staff had included such remarkable photographers as Walker Evans, Dorothea Lange, Russell Lee, Arthur Rothstein, and Jack Delano; by the time the agency was disbanded in 1942 they had made more than 250,000 photographs of American life. Unlike the photographs Burke had seen in *The Family of Man,* which had been used to illustrate archetypes and platitudes, the pictures in "Just Before the War" recorded the dense particularities of American life. If *The Family of Man* was like a sermon, then "Just Before the War" was a visual replica of the contents of an American Noah's ark. There were pictures of slums and farmhouse parlors, black bars in Chicago and trailer parks in L.A.; there were car wrecks, soda jerks, and old widow ladies; city streets, seashores, and sideshows; there were migrants, jobless men, and Jim Crow blacks. Everywhere there were cars. In particular there were the photographs of Russell Lee, a man who once set out with his camera on a six-week assignment and didn't return for nine months; a traveler who'd developed his film in the bathrooms of cheap hotels; a photographer who'd made pictures of anything and anyone with the simple clarity of a man entranced.

Burke looked at the show and felt a road running through it and past him, straight to the horizon. He believed that only one other man had traveled it in the twenty years since the staff of the FSA had done its work. That man was a Swiss émigré, a protégé of Walker Evans, a man named Robert Frank. Shortly before Burke had been confused by Sommer's dead coyotes, a friend had shown him a copy of *The Americans,* a book of pictures Frank had made after a journey across the United States in the late fifties. It was a book of movement and dread; of highways, cars, TV's, bars, urinals, and diners; of American flags and jukeboxes; of blacks by the riverside and whites trapped in luncheonettes; of grotesque politicians, gamblers, and socialites; and of lovely young men who slept under trees, ate in cafeterias, and sat in obscure parks, waiting for salvation and looking for love. It was a work of pain, death, boredom, and loneliness, and although Burke tried, at first, to dismiss it as neither uplifting nor transcendent, he could no more escape it than he could avoid his own past.

In Burke's second year of graduate school, Frank was a visiting lecturer, telling stories about taking chances. His friends were Allen Ginsberg and Jack Kerouac. To make *The Americans,* he had sacrificed his marriage and his family, and, once having made the book, he'd abandoned photography and became a film-maker. He was a restless man who loved to head in the opposite direction. Students asked him his opinion of other photographers, and he dismissed most of them as irrelevant. All that mattered, he said, was taking whatever chances were necessary to discover one's vision and pursue one's art. Even the simplest things, he said, were matters of life and death. '"You wave down a cab, and you get in. The guy looks at you, and, first of all, what's on his mind is "Is this guy crazy and is he gonna kill me?' The first exchange is life and death."

At the beginning of *The Plague,* Tarrou had written in his journal: "*Query:* How to contrive not to waste one's time? *Answer:* By being fully aware of it all the while. *Ways in which this can be done:* By spending one's days in an uneasy chair in a dentist's waiting room; by . . . listening to lectures in a language one doesn't understand; by travelling by the longest and least convenient train routes and, of course, standing all the way. . . ." Like Tarrou, Frank, the émigré, had sat in uncomfortable places, listened to incomprehensible speeches, and traveled the long way 'round. All the while he had, like Tarrou, remained alert, thinking of matters of life and death. But unlike Tarrou, who had taken notes, Frank had taken pictures. Burke began to dream about him. He still does. Even now, when Burke has completed a body of work, Frank appears every

once in a while in his dreams to look at Burke's pictures. Frank, the risk taker, traveler, and chance maker, the stranger whose code is comprehension, became, for Burke, "the most important spiritual father I've got."

In due time Burke was graduated from the Rhode Island School of Design and found a job teaching photography at the School of Fine Arts of the Boston Museum. Boston seemed a civilized place, a city of educated youth whose major industries were education and high technology. In certain districts the oldest inhabitants were twenty-eight-year-old graduate students, the clerks in the drugstores had B.A.'s in Oriental civilization, and the waitresses talked of moving to Colorado. It was a city with traditions of reticent calm, polite gentility, and historical preservation that were only occasionally disrupted by helpless spasms of working-class rage. Except for what happened in Roxbury and Southy, it was a city of paper chases behind closed doors. Burke found a loft in a decrepit industrial district of an obscure suburb, fell in love with the diamond cutter's daughter, and grew uneasy. There was always fine coffee, fresh fish, and imported beer; there were always games of handball and dinners at Burmese restaurants, but nothing of any consequence broke loose in public. The city's students lived either in the future or in the provisional present; the engineers, analysts, and consultants spent their time in cubicles solving problems set by management committees. Some citizens argued about matters of taste, others about matters of conscience, but no one lived on the edge. Burke grew bored and then desperate. During lulls in conversation he'd invite his guests to join him while he fired a few rounds at the silhouette he'd nailed to his wall. He thought of placing newspaper ads for models with scars. Then, in 1975, his old fraternity buddy Hower, the open-faced, average-looking guy with the ring in his ear, told him about the Kentucky photographic project. Burke signed on, feeling like a man who'd just been saved from the lotus-eaters.

During a semester break he and the diamond cutter's daughter and his dog, Ralph, drove to Louisville and met Hower and his dog, Blackwall. They all climbed into Hower's '49 Hudson and set out on a tour of eastern Kentucky. Whenever they stopped, it was as if a circus had arrived. Everywhere people smiled, stared at the car, and asked questions.

A few months later Burke returned for another visit. This time he drove his old Volvo station wagon through the mountains, accompanied by a man who'd been his friend and neighbor when they were boys. His friend had gone to Harvard Divinity School, dropped out, gone to Barnum & Bailey Clown School, became a disciple of Maher Baba, and traveled to India. He'd returned, dressed in white, his hair long and curly, his beard down to his chest. He sat next to Burke in a dhoti, while they drove through the Kentucky coal-fields in a car whose silver roof and gray, green, white, and blue body panels were the result of purchases made at different wrecking yards whenever the consequences of rust and accident required a more permanent remedy than masking tape. During the trip Burke and his friend stopped in Pikeville, at a general store whose walls were covered with old signs. Burke's friend walked up to the building in his robe and began taking pictures. The owners came out and told him they didn't like his manners, his looks, his clothes, or his camera. Then they walked him back to the car and told him and Burke to get lost. Burke knew enough about the photographer Russell Lee's sympathy, patience, and respectful manners to understand his friend's mistake; he had also read enough of *Deliverance* not to argue.

Once he got back to Boston, he peeled off his "Nuclear Vacationland" bumper sticker and used a brush to paint his whole car the color of a silver radiator. He understood enough about small country towns to know that if a photographer pulled in, he'd become the afternoon's entertainment. Since there was no way to take pictures and be invisible, one solution was to be so obvious that no one felt threatened. A Volvo painted like a B-24 was a perfect solution. Another solution was to use a variety of black-and-white Polaroid film that produced an instant picture as well as a negative that could be made permanent if it were dipped in a pail of sodium sulfite solution. Burke planned to drive into a town, draw a crowd, take pictures, peel away the paper, and then hand out the prints like the Lone Ranger giving out silver bullets. The people would have their portraits. Burke would have his negatives, and he could ride off in a cloud of dust and amused goodwill. He christened his car the Silver Bullet, strung it with charms and a bumper sticker that said, "God Is My Copilot," and began his travels.

What he discovered was a country and a people so different from anything he'd known that the more of it he experienced, the more he wondered if he was still in the United States. Every few months he'd return to Boston, lock himself in his darkroom, and make work prints from the negatives he'd made in the field. Then his friends would visit, and he'd tell them road stories. Some would listen and smile like polite children who considered themselves too old for fairy tales. Others would fall off their chairs in disbelief. To begin with, there were the obvious things like the guns and the cars. In Massachusetts guns were forbidden objects; in Kentucky they were as common as shovels and as visible as flags and crucifixes. In Massachusetts the freezes, thaws, and road salt of winter changed cars into things that resembled the vital organs of cancer patients; in the winter rains of Kentucky, immaculate '57 Chevrolets squealed around corners, driven by men who had dreamed of owning them when they were boys. Beyond the weapons that functioned in Burke's pictures as "symbols of the craziness and foreignness of the place" and the Chevies he used as visual elements in pictures of adult male teenage fantasy, there were the manners of the people themselves. Unlike the reticent and circumspect citizens of Boston, the people Burke met were, at best, open and hospitable and, at worst, vulnerable and unprotected. Many of them had spent their lives on farms at the ends of hollers or in the mines; some had been in the army; others had worked in Chicago or Cincinnati and then returned, feeling as if they had been tricked and insulted by people beneath contempt. Everyone watched television and wanted what was in the commercials. Some became coal operators and, by a combination of good luck and simple cunning, became rich by literally digging the ground out from under their own feet. Without fully knowing what they were doing except spending their money, they leveled the tops of small mountains and built houses with mansard roofs whose interiors looked like funeral homes and bordellos. Occasionally, wandering around through all this, were congenital idiots, cretins, dwarfs, and schizophrenics, who, in New

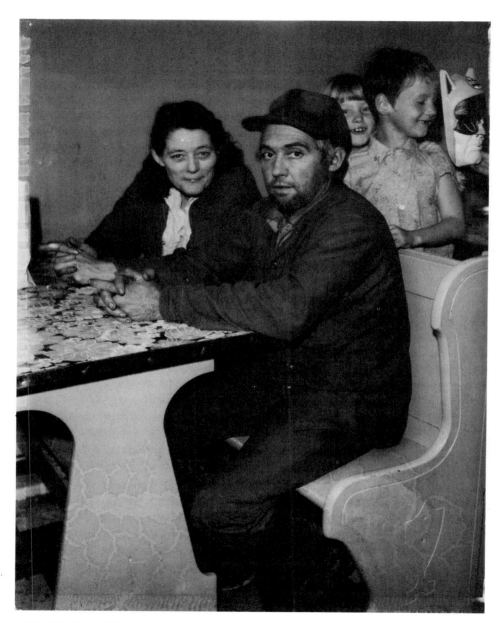

CARROLLTON, KENTUCKY, 1975

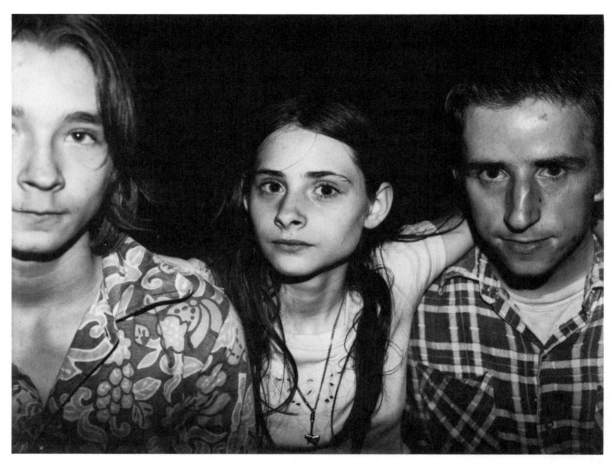

McDOWELL COUNTY, WEST VIRGINIA, 1979

England, would have been kept in institutions.

For a photographer like Burke, who believed in the symbolic meaning of appearances, anyplace where things were out in the open was better than a place, no matter how civilized, where meanings hid behind traditional masks. He began to spend longer and longer periods of time in Kentucky, alone on the road except for Ralph and an occasional pint of George Dickle. The place fascinated him not just because its people were either too kindhearted or too naïve to hide themselves from his scrutiny but because nearly everyone and everything he saw bore marks as recognizable as those of the subway riders whom James Agee had described in *Many Are Called*. For sixty years the land and the people of eastern Kentucky had been ruthlessly exploited as if they had been the chattels of a nineteenth-century European power. The land was ravaged, cleft, and riddled. The people, for all their innocence and kindness, were as marred and scarred as the patients in *Mortal Lessons*. Burke kept taking pictures of them, looking for signs of grace.

Compared with New England, Kentucky was a raw frontier. In Massachusetts the universities and the computer and electronics firms spawned a secular life of the mind; in Kentucky the only abstractions were the heaven and hell of the fundamentalist churches. In Boston fortunes were made by electrical or optical engineers turned inventors and entrepreneurs; in Kentucky even the very rich of Lexington maintained themselves by breeding, birthing, and trading large animals. Kentucky was a place of pungent, corporeal reality where things figurative were less important than things literal. It was a place of objects and gestures. It was also a place so ravaged by a confluence of greed, innocence, need, and availability that to an alert traveler, it resembled a moral and sociological Grand Canyon, where layers of extreme wealth and poverty, waste and scarcity, independence and vulnerability could be seen, almost at once, in a single glance. Occasionally the miners of the region would go on strike, and the place, which already looked, here and there, as if it had been bombed from the air, would become an actual combat zone. Under these circumstances there was always the chance that if Burke weren't very alert and very careful, he might make a mistake as difficult to recover from as a bad motorcycle accident. That possibility spawned an edge he had experienced before.

There were situations that appeared to him so strange and deadly but so innocuous—"the fear was just in people's yards," he said—that sometimes he'd be too frightened to leave his car. Too many of those, too close together, kept him in bed in a ratty motel room, unable to bear "*another* town square of people staring at me." But as a photographer whose terrain was the social landscape, he knew that his art depended

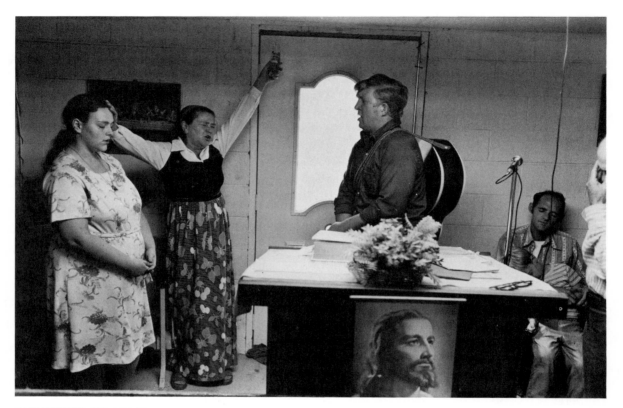

VALLEY VIEW, KENTUCKY, 1976

JOLO, WEST VIRGINIA, 1979

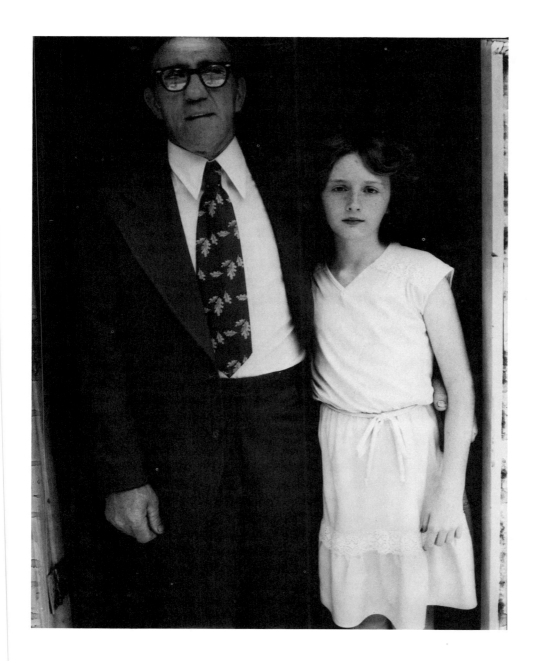

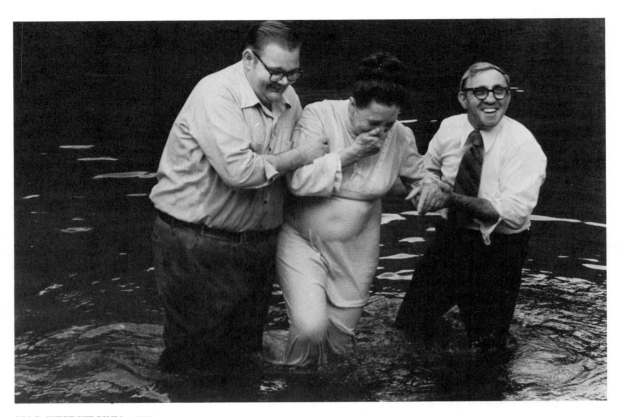

JOLO, WEST VIRGINIA, 1979

on intense and unpredictable situations that were within and, at the same time, beyond his control. Up to a point, the more variables there were, ricocheting around like billiard balls at a break, then the more coincidences, and the better his photographs, as long as he kept his wits about him. He began to use fear like a muse: The more unfamiliar a situation was, the more frightened he became; the more frightened he was, the more alert he became; the more alert he was, the more aware he became of the point at which the configuration of the world matched the scars of his heart. At that moment, when he drew the world in and the world drew him out, he made his picture in middle breath.

He used to hang out around whirlpools, places like Churchill Downs, and Keeneland, where all the extremes of poverty and depravity, wealth and degeneracy, skill, chance, hope, and animal beauty smashed up and around each other. He used to set up his tripod and wait for the jockeys on their way to the saddling circle. He'd watch them after the races, cocky little Dominicans in flashy clothes, driving flashy cars, greeted by Vanderbilts and invited by Whitneys.

Once he walked into a bathhouse that had been turned into an apostolic church. The first thing he saw was two young guys repairing an electric guitar on the altar. There were tools and wires, a picture of Jesus, and a bottle of Mazola that the minister used to anoint those who came forward during the service. The entire congregation consisted of one clan. He spent a few days there, and they thanked God for sending him.

One day, toward evening, he stopped to talk to a young guy who was standing on the road next to his '57 Chevy. Burke had been photographing every '57 he saw, just as he'd been photographing everyone with eye damage and every woman with curlers. He asked about the car, and the kid told him where he could buy one. The kid had a cross around his neck, and no shirt on. Burke took a picture, and they talked some more. It was getting dark. The kid told him he was a jealous man and that he had a little wife at home. Then he asked Burke if he wanted to see his house. Burke said sure. It turned out to be a nice little house. They walked in, and there, on the bed, reading a paperback of *Charlie's Angels*, was an eighteen-year-old blonde in cutoffs and a Little Orphan Annie T-shirt. Next to her, where her husband slept, was his gun. On the wall was a heart from a box of Valentine's candy. Burke was frightened to look, so he took a picture. The kid said he'd show him his hawk in the morning. Burke said he'd spend the night in his car.

Later on he met a black, blind-in-one-eye tenant farmer who was known for his fiddling. His favorite song was "The Tennessee Waltz." Burke spent enough time drinking and talking with him so that, when Thanksgiving came and the diamond cutter's daughter said she could fly down

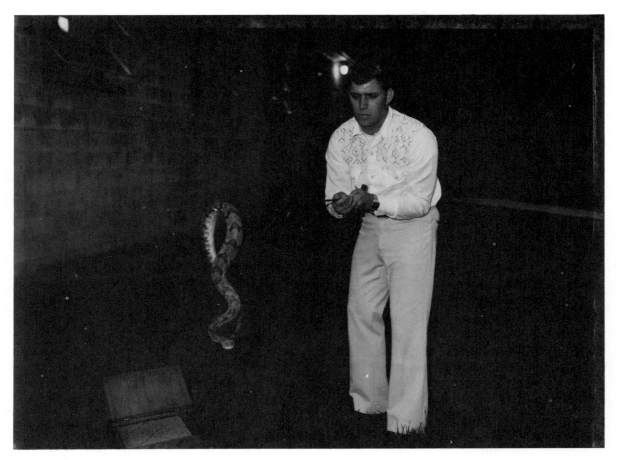

LEGO, WEST VIRGINIA, 1979

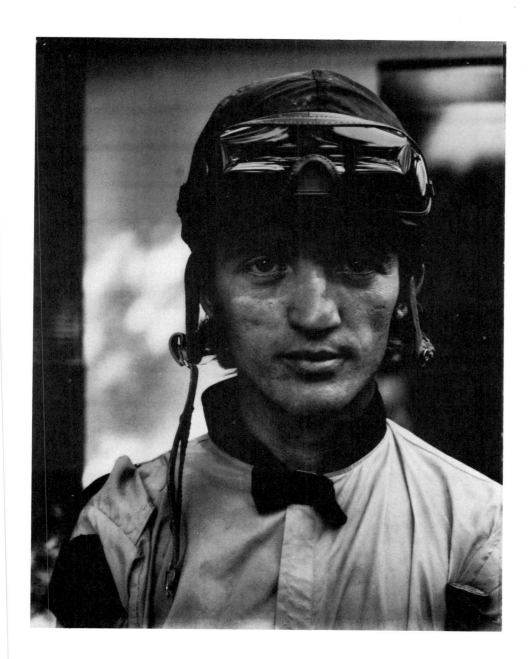

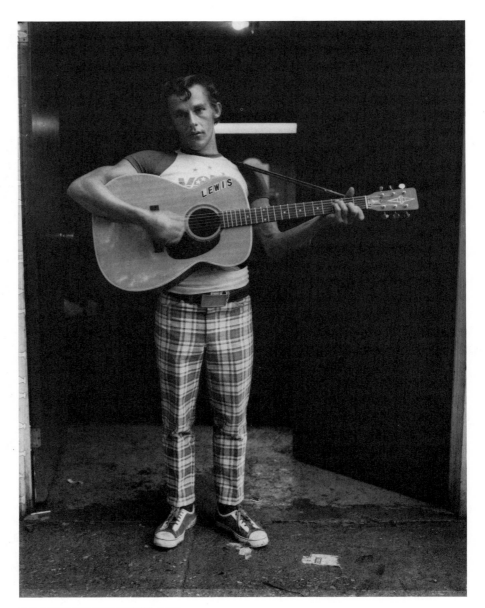

VALLEY VIEW, KENTUCKY, 1976

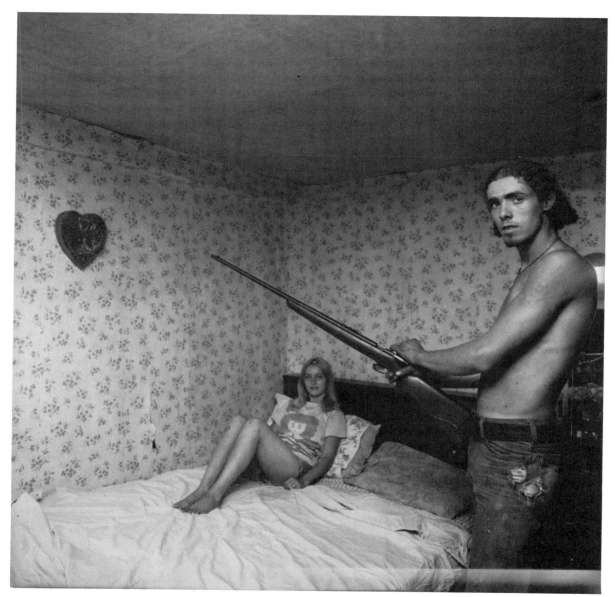

EASTERN KENTUCKY, 1977

for two days, Burke asked the man if the two of them could share Thanksgiving dinner with him. The man said, sure, come along. Burke anticipated a warm, traditional, picturesque farm dinner. When they got there, there was no food, only whiskey. Everybody got loaded. Burke kept taking pictures of the fiddler, sawing away at "The Tennessee Waltz," but he was too drunk to remember to dunk his Polaroids in sodium sulfite. In the meantime, the fiddler tried to seduce his girl. In the print Burke eventually made from one of the ruined negatives, luminous smoke and rays of light shone and billowed from the side of the fiddler's head and his bow, while, at his feet, a little blond girl sat bewitched by the waltz.

Burke kept a diary which he filled with doodles, scratches, and scribbles whenever something remarkable happened. In one week in the middle of July during his second year of travel, things started happening, one after the other, like cherries thudding into place in a slot machine. To begin with, he summoned up his courage and introduced himself to the Cleeves during the annual yearling sales at Keeneland. The Cleeves were remarkably successful and wealthy horse breeders whose Picture Book Farm was so idyllic a place that the manufacturers of various brands of mentholated cigarettes had used it, again and again over the years, as a backdrop for their ads of green and carefree pleasure. Burke had been told that the Cleeves col-

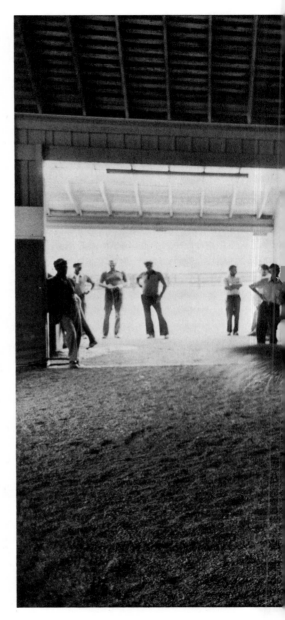

FAYETTE COUNTY, KENTUCKY, 1977

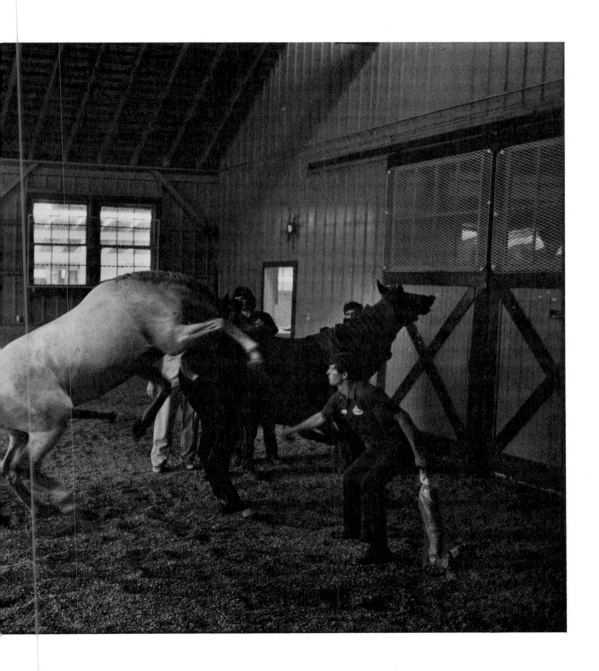

lected people: Sturgis preferred basketball and football stars from the state university; Marilyn preferred hairdressers and show business personalities who appeared on "Hollywood Squares" when they weren't performing in Reno. Occasionally, the Cleeves gave parties to which they invited several hundred people whom they entertained with sword swallowers and contortionists. During the parties there was always a ceremony at which the couple presented gifts to each other. Burke had heard that at the last one, Marilyn had given Sturgis a girl painted gold, and Sturgis had given Marilyn a boa constrictor. It was said that the couple kept forever young with the help of various medical therapies and surgical innovations.

Burke had heard these and many more things about the Cleeves, who kept an unusually high public profile, but he had been frightened to approach them not only because they seemed larger than life but because he imagined that they and their retinue were probably sophisticated enough to accuse him of being what he actually was: a spy. The second day of the yearling sales he wandered through the horse barns at Keeneland, past canopied benches, free Coke machines, and young blondes in blazers escorted by middle-aged men who'd arrived in limousines with diplomatic plates. He took a picture of one of the Hunt brothers in a rumpled shirt, shaking hands with an admirer, while next to him stood a bodyguard who kept his eyes on the stranger's face. Burke had heard that the Cleeves had converted a tack room into a screening room where they entertained clients and showed films extolling the heart and courage of their studs and the promise of their yearlings. When he got close to it, Burke asked a lady where he could find Marilyn. She smiled, took him to a door, and announced him. Burke stepped out of the sunlight and heat into a cool, utterly dark room that smelled of hay, saddles, horse medicine, and Marilyn's perfume. Her scent was so strong and so characteristic that later, at a party where there were so many people Burke couldn't see, he was able to locate Marilyn with his nose. Just before the door to the screening room closed, he caught sight of her: breasts like honeydews covered in white crochet, wearing large sunglasses whose lenses were set with her initials in rhinestones. Her voice was soft and drowsy. She introduced him to a half dozen men; Burke groped for their hands in the dark. A few of them were owners. One of them was a world-famous trainer; when Burke didn't catch his name and asked again, no one laughed. Someone handed him a gin and tonic, and he sat back. At that moment Sturgis walked in and turned on all the lights.

The room was lined with mirrors and draped in pink. There were a dozen chairs, a cassette player, two silver champagne buckets, a perfume atomizer, a backgammon board, and two fiber-optic lamps. Beyond the room were the barns where the yearlings stood, waiting to be taken before an audience of millionaires, seated in a nearby pavilion. Sturgis had come in to get a drink. Burke had heard that he had the habit of pouring whiskey into his hand and lighting it, but Sturgis just walked over to the slot cut in the wall for the projection booth, leaned into it, and ordered a G and T. Seated in front of him, her back to the wall, her head a few inches from his belly, was a middle-aged blonde. Sturgis leaned into her as if she weren't there. She looked away, and he reached into the booth for his drink. Then he turned out the lights, and everyone watched a film of a stud called Betamax impregnating a mare. Sturgis left in the middle of it. When it was over, Burke asked Marilyn for permission to visit and photograph them the next day. She said he could do anything he wanted. All he had to do was ask. Burke thanked her, she smiled, and he took a few pictures.

The next day he drove through the gates of Picture Book Farm, down an avenue of oaks, past ponds and fields bordered with fences whose white lines rose and fell across the swell of the land. When he got out of the car, he looked across, and far in the distance a herd of black horses rushed out from behind a grove of trees. Sturgis came down the steps to greet him. Marilyn, he said, was indisposed, but there was a game of croquet just starting if he cared to join them. Burke hadn't played since he was ten years old. He soon discovered that Sturgis and his friends played croquet with each other the way the Queen of Hearts and her court had played it in Wonderland. Before Burke knew what had happened, one of Sturgis's friends had sent Burke's ball flying into the woods, where Burke spent the next half hour looking for it. In the meantime, Sturgis won and was greeted by cries of amazement and congratulations, as if he had just swum the Channel. Since Burke couldn't find his ball in the brush, Sturgis charitably suggested a walk instead of a rematch. They were halfway to one of the barns when Sturgis looked at Burke and then smacked him on the forehead. "Well, Bill," he said, "I don't want you to take this wrong, but you had a *fly* on your forehead." Then he wiped the fly off his hand with his finger and rubbed it on Burke's sleeve. When they returned, Sturgis wrapped a white silk scarf around his neck, changed into a beautifully tailored black leather motorcycle jacket, and ordered his police Harley wheeled out of the garage. Burke took a few pictures of him, leaning against it in his calfskin boots and his aviator glasses. That night Burke went to a party where Marilyn gave Sturgis a stuffed sabertooth tiger, and Sturgis gave Marilyn a cageful of minks.

A few days later Burke drove east, into Martin County, heading for Inez, the county seat. He'd noticed that the farther east he went in a state, "the crazier things got." Martin County was so far east that if he'd fallen asleep at the wheel, he'd have ended up in West Virginia. A couple of miles outside Inez, he picked up a kid wearing a Cat hat. The kid said he was on his way to work at the carnival in town. He'd been to Chicago but come back "'cause there're too many niggers there." He told Burke about "Nigger Holler," where "they lynched three niggers. Any niggers come to Martin County, they kill 'em. The judge has somebody do it." Burke dropped the kid off at the fair and drove to "Nigger Holler," but all he saw were coal trucks and bad roads. He kept on driving until he got to the town of Lovely, where he postmarked some postcards, then kept on going until he reached Beauty, where he postmarked some more. On the way back he stopped in a country store. While he was talking with the lady behind the counter, a guy came in all in a sweat, and said, "Sorry to interrupt you, Ethel, but I got a hurt dog up at the house. I shot him by accident. Now I'm outta shells, and he's hurt real bad. You got any twenty-two shorts?" Burke offered him a ride, but he had one. After he had left, Burke and Ethel spent a half hour bargaining over a half roll of masking tape and a beer cooler.

He decided to camp with the carny people outside town. Burke walked up to a bumper car ride and started blasting away with his strobe. The operators asked him for pictures and introduced themselves. One was Burl; the other, Ernie. Burl said he and his wife hauled the whole ride, cars and all, in a semi and then lived in the trailer after they'd set up at a fair. He invited Burke to a party after the ride had shut down for the night. The party was in the semi. There was a sleeping platform, some dirty blankets, and a TV set; the floor was littered with empty Coleman fuel cans. There were no windows. The place smelled like onions, bologna, and marijuana. There were eight or nine carnies smoking out of a hookah filled with Scope mouthwash, listening to heavy metal rock and roll blasting out of some cheap speakers. The sounds of a vicious, spectacular thunderstorm cut through the music, but the doors of the trailer stayed closed. Burl decided to provide a light show. He found a plastic dry-cleaning bag, knotted it, hung it from a coat hanger over a pail of water, and then lit it. Blue, flaming blobs of plastic hit the water with a ZPPPP. The storm grew worse, and the whole place filled with black, poisonous smoke. Burke took a few pictures.

After everyone had left, he and Ernie and Burl sat and counted tickets from the ride. Burl insisted that Burke join them for a bologna and cheese sandwich. It was three o'clock in the morning; neither Burl nor Ernie had eaten all day; by the time Ernie found a knife and a loaf of bunny bread and made everyone sandwiches, he had mayonnaise behind his ears. He told Burke he'd wanted to be a coal truck driver. He'd been an army sergeant and taught truck driving to cadets at West Point. He'd just loved it when they called him sir. He said his favorite song was about a raccoon-hunting monkey. Burke was too far gone to say anything but "What?" So Ernie told him:

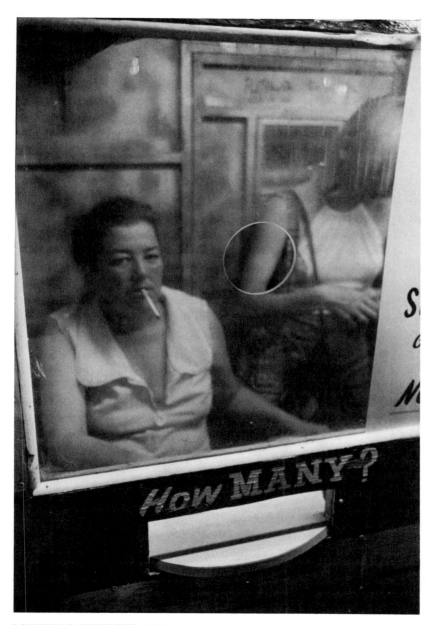

LOUISVILLE, KENTUCKY, 1975

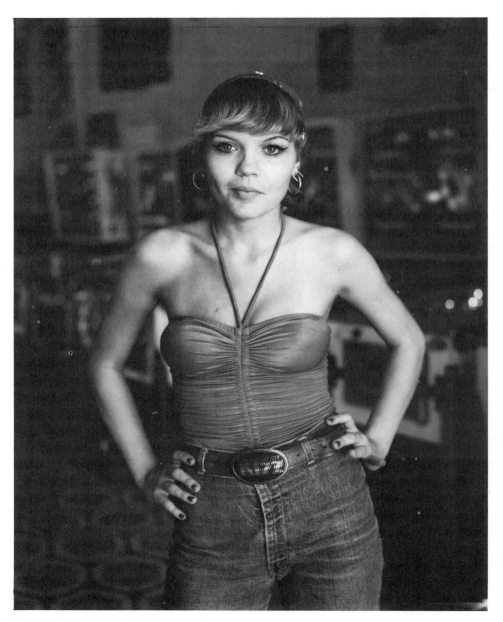

WILLIAMSBURG, WEST VIRGINIA, 1979

"There's this monkey, see, who hates coons with a passion and never misses. The fellow who owns him tries to sell him to his friend. One night he takes his friend out hunting with the monkey. The guy's dog trees a coon. The monkey goes up with a flashlight in one hand and a forty-five in the other. He stays up there a while, but nothing happens. Then he comes down. And shoots the dog. The guy who's trying to sell him says to his friend, 'Oh! I forgot to tell ya. The only thing the monkey hates worse than a coon is a lyin' dog.'" Burl started laughing with a mouthful of bologna and cheese. Burke tried to take a picture, but his strobe was dead. He said good night, stumbled out of the semi, and went to sleep in the back of his car.

Burke was on the road by seven the next morning. The day before, on his way to Beauty, he'd seen a camper on a pickup truck with a big red star painted on it parked off the road by a creek. He decided he'd drive back and take some pictures. He slowed down as he approached the pickup again. Then he saw a man with a heavy bandage around his head, crouching by the side of the road. The man frightened him. He didn't move, didn't look up, didn't change his expression. He looked like a lizard asleep in the sun. Heavy eyelids; three or four days' growth of beard. Maybe forty years old. Wearing a white short-sleeve shirt, plastered to him by the morning heat. Even driving by, Burke was scared by his looks. He drove up the road, turned

around, and headed back. The man never looked up. Burke turned around again, drove past, and pulled off. He took out his camera and pretended to photograph a swinging bridge, fifty yards down the creek. As he was adjusting his equipment, a man climbed out of the camper. Burke shouted to him, "Is it OK if I photograph the bridge?"

The man shouted back, "Sure. Help yourself. They're kin to me." Then he and the guy with the bandage walked across another bridge and disappeared into a house. Burke killed some time. After ten minutes one of the men shouted across, "How's it going?" Burke said it was going OK. He kept on doing nothing, going through the motions in the heat, waiting. Just when he'd decided he'd have to try something else, they came out and crossed the bridge. This time there was a third guy with them. This one was a little older, very thin, with a short, pineapple haircut, and as he came closer, Burke saw he had no teeth. They all gathered around.

Burke asked them who lived in the camper. Then he asked the Lizard what happened to his head. The guy said he'd been down in the camper, screwing the woman who lived there. There'd been a couple of kids and a white dog running around. Then her husband had come home. He was drunk. He found a chain and hit the Lizard with it. Cut his head to the bone and hurt his eye. He went to the hospital and waited for the doctor to sew him up, but the doctor never came. So a nurse bandaged him and gave him some pain pills. That was two days ago. The pills were loose and turning to paste in his pocket, his eye was damaged, and his skull was split open. All he hoped, he said, was that he ran into the son of a bitch out in the woods during deer season. All Burke wanted was to take his picture.

It was a dry county, but Burke had beer in his car. He offered them some; they finished it quickly. Then he took some pictures. After that they started looking very seriously at the contents of his car. Burke thought they were trying to decide what they wanted. They kept telling Burke he ought to go down and take a picture of the woman in the camper. He would have loved to, but he was afraid that even if the lady's husband didn't blow him away, his three new friends would relieve him of his possessions in his absence. Some of the pictures he'd taken looked good, but the guys weren't leaving. Burke was getting scared. He still had a pint of George Dickle in the car. He suggested they share it. The only trouble, he said, was that the booze was hot. He asked if they had any ice. The Lizard and his friend dispatched Maynard, the old guy with the pineapple haircut, to get something cold. Maynard came back with one can of grape and one can of orange soda. The guys chugalugged the bourbon until they'd finished half the bottle; then they poured in some orange and some grape to cool it off. And then they just de-

molished it. The Lizard and Maynard wandered off to find some shade. Burke packed his gear as fast as he could, said thanks, and left.

By then it was noon, and he was not only drunk but wired. He drove for a while to settle down. He'd almost lost it back by the camper. The creek ran into a river, and he followed it. He decided to take a few pictures of the landscape to relax. No lizards or pineapple heads, just a view, properly framed. He saw a group of houses up on a hill overlooking the river and drove up. All the houses were crowded on top of one another. There was one in particular that stood out at a crazy angle. It had homemade signs in the front yard that said "Reverend Berry's Church." He drove by it once and then again. The third time he passed, an old woman and a young one stood screaming at each other in the front yard. Burke turned around in a cemetery, and when he returned, the old woman had collapsed and was being carried inside. He kept on going and found a store that sold bread and meat and tomatoes. He asked the little girl behind the counter who the Reverend Berry was; she said he was crazy. Burke went back.

He didn't know what excuse to make, so he just knocked on the door. A big man with a grave face, a huge belly, and no teeth answered. Burke forgot what he was going to say. The man looked down at him from a height. Burke said something about the State Bicentennial Commission

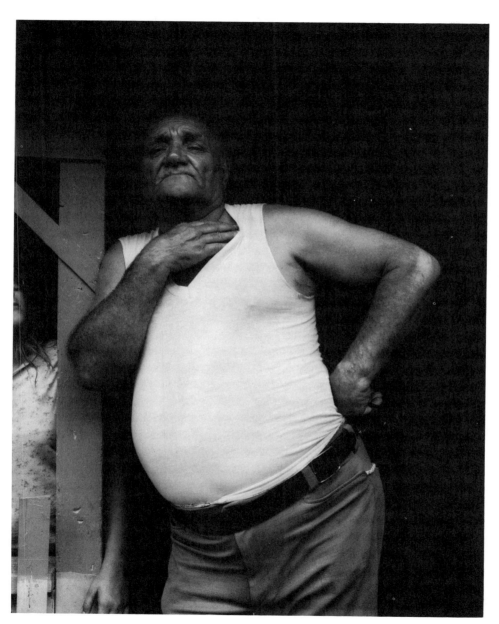

BELVEDERE, OHIO, 1979

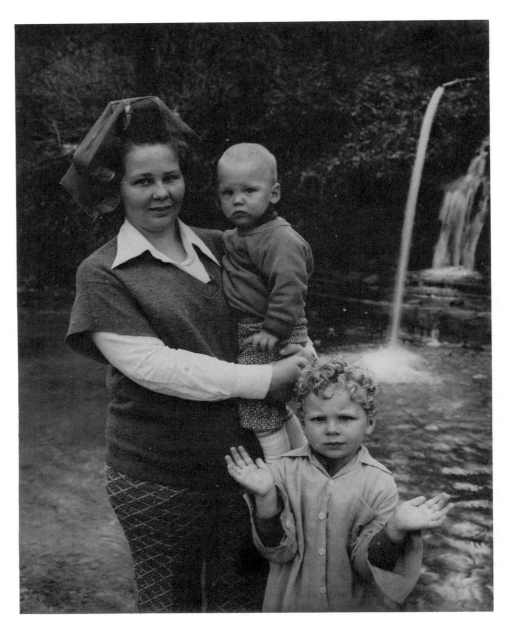

VANCEBURG, KENTUCKY, 1976

and how he was photographing a lot of churches and asked if he could have permission to photograph this one. The Reverend Berry told him to step in. Burke couldn't understand what was happening. The Lizard and his friends had temporarily rendered him incapable of coherent thought or discourse. All he wanted was to photograph the outside of the house. The Reverend Berry explained that his wife had just had a heart attack, and who had Burke said he was? Burke said he'd been passing by when he'd seen her collapse and that he was sorry. The Reverend Berry said she was all right now, he'd cured her before when she'd had cancer, and he would cure her again. He said he would ask God if it was all right for Burke to take pictures. He closed his eyes and didn't say anything for a while. Then he asked Burke to accompany him into the tabernacle. The tabernacle was one room of his four-room house. It was fifteen feet square. The reverend said he could get fourteen people in it. There was a little platform and a cross made of two pink Styrofoam egg cartons. At the bottom of each egg cup was a large red Magic Marker dot. There were little crosses painted in strange places on the ceiling, in the corners, and on the walls. On a shelf above the altar was a little wooden box. Burke asked what was in it. The Reverend

said, "I don't want you to take offense, but since you asked it, it must be God's will." He opened the box and took out a vial of oil. Then he put his arm around Burke, held him tight, and anointed him. As the oil ran down his face, the Reverend put his thumbs between Burke's eyes and pressed down hard. It was the same spot Sturgis had chosen to kill a fly. Slapped by a rich man and anointed by a preacher. Right between the eyes. All in five days. Burke took a picture of the Reverend standing on the porch. Then they hugged each other, and Burke drove away.

That night Burke wrote it all down in his diary, from Sturgis and Ernie to the Lizard and the Reverend. He didn't look at it again until months later, back in Boston, when he printed their pictures. And he didn't think about it too much until he read it out to me, the night we sat, me with my eye patched and my feet on the stove, him sipping, walking, and talking. I couldn't help myself then. I said, "It sounds like a goddamn parable. Who do you think you are?" Burke didn't say anything. The hearts and the cupids and the lightning bolts hung from the ceiling and twirled in the heat from the stove. I kept waiting for an answer until I smelled the soles of my shoes burning. Burke just smiled and kept on walking.

There were four John McWilliamses. The first one dug gold in California and marched with Sherman to the sea. The second was a banker, investor, and philanthropist who once owned most of the San Fernando Valley. The third was a manufacturer who longed to farm the land. And the fourth was a photographer who, in his own way, did what his great-grandfather had done long ago.

A few years before the First World War, when the very first John McWilliams was an old man, he wrote a book, *His Youth, Experiences in California, and the Civil War.* Princeton University Press handsomely printed and bound 100 copies of it for the sake of his children and their descendants. Forty years later his great-grandson, the photographer, took a copy of it from his father's library without asking since the old man's stories were as much his inheritance as his genes.

The old man had written that *his* great-grandfather, a man named Alexander, had been born in the middle of the Atlantic Ocean, on board a ship bound from Scotland to America. Alexander's parents settled for a time in southwestern Pennsylvania and then moved farther west into Ohio. There, when Alexander came of age, he married a woman of Irish Protestant descent who bore him three sons and then died a year after the birth of her last child. That child was named James; in his turn, James was to marry and father John, the old man who wrote his recollections for the sake of his offspring. John wrote that his two uncles, his father James's brothers, had taken a flatboat to New Orleans, loaded with grain from their father's mill and whiskey from his distillery, but had never returned, either killed by cholera or murdered by robbers. Their deaths not only broke their father's heart but ruined him. Alexander sold everything he owned, moved farther into Ohio, and, at the age of sixty-five, died on newly cleared land.

In 1824 James married Margaret Latimer, a woman of Welsh descent. She bore him five children and managed to live for fifteen years after the wedding. In 1834 James left his family and traveled by steamboat down the Ohio, up the Mississippi, and then up the Illinois in search of new land. Near the very center of Illinois, he discovered a colony of New Englanders and resolved to settle there. He returned to Ohio, sold his farm, and loaded his family onto a steamboat. As soon as they were on board, his children contracted scarlet fever. The steamer managed to travel as far as Naples, Illinois, before it was frozen in the ice. There on board the boat caught in the middle of the river, James and Margaret's daughter Rachel died. James walked ashore, bought a house, and then buried the child. A month later he bought 250 acres of land and timber in the nearby town of Griggsville Prairie. A few years after that, when he returned to Naples to dig up the bones of his daughter and bury them on his own land, he discovered that the river had washed away her grave.

John was three years old when his family settled on the prairie. There were buffalo bones scattered everywhere, and wolves howled in the night. Until his mother died, the family lived in a cabin lit only by hand-dipped candles and the bright flames of hickory logs. Food was cooked and bread was baked in iron pots nestled in or hung above the coals. The family had chairs, beds, a mirror framed with gilt, and a clock with wooden gears which they had brought with them from Ohio. They ate only with knives. They raised, killed, and cured their own pigs. They hunted rabbits, quail, and grouse. They gathered wild strawberries, raspberries, blackberries, plums, and wild grapes. They ate hazelnuts, pecans, walnuts, and three kinds of hickory nuts. Turnips they ate like fruit. Tomatoes they called love apples and set on the mantelpiece to be admired but not eaten. Once or twice they found hollow trees full of wild honey, which they carted away in tubs. Every fall millions of wild pigeons, migrating south, turned the sky black for four days. At night, when the birds roosted in the woods, the settlers fired shotguns into the trees and, at daybreak, hauled away wagonloads of them.

When John was six, his father bought more land, planted it in wheat, dug his own well, and was elected to the state legislature. The same year the family's youngest child, a girl named Mary, fell down the new well, and although she was rescued alive, the shock of the accident soon killed her mother, who had never recovered from the death of her other daughter on the ice-bound boat. A year after she died, James married a New England schoolteacher named Lucretia Prescott, the daughter of a judge from Massachusetts. James moved his family into town, where Lucretia taught her stepchildren manners, dosed them with cod-liver oil, and dressed the boys in collars. Two years after the move, safe in town, John's oldest brother died of pneumonia. The town made John "crazy to go back to the farm. I would run away and go out there. When I was 14, I hired out to a man to drive a team of 8 oxen to break up the raw prairie. . . . I worked for him for 3 or 4 months."

When John was sixteen, his father began to trade lumber for corn and potatoes and send the produce by towboat to Chicago. The same year John began to read about the goldfields of California. In the winter of his seventeenth year, while he and his father were trimming trees in the orchard, John said, "Father, I'm going to California even if I have to run away. I'm going or die." James had already lost two brothers, a daughter, a wife, and an eldest son. He

wasn't anxious to lose another. John was more than six feet tall, as thin as a rail, and shaking with fever dreams of the golden West. James had no choice.

In the April of 1849 John and three other boys set out in a wagon, drawn by four teams of oxen, headed for California. James went by steamer to St. Louis, bought guns and provisions, and met the boys with the supplies in St. Joseph, Missouri. He pleaded with his son to come home. John said he'd rather die. So James gave him two English sovereigns and two $5 gold pieces and told him to save them for the last. He didn't tell him that along with the bacon and the sugar, neatly folded next to the axes, shovels, pans, and picks, he had packed his son's burial shroud. Three years later, when John returned to Griggsville via Panama and New Orleans, he had lost the shroud but he had gained thirty pounds and still had one of the gold pieces in his pocket. "I can say I owe my life to a change of climate and living and to fat bacon instead of cod liver oil."

Far to the west the Mexican War had just ended; in the East there was a depression. That year 24,000 people crossed the plains, dreaming of gold. Lines of wagons, drawn up, wagon tongue to rear axle, as many as twelve oxen harnessed to each, stretched for miles and miles, waiting in a line that crept forward day and night to the ferries that carried them across the Missouri. John and his wagon of boys were among them. Once across, they joined a company of 100 people in twenty-five wagons, every one of them from Pike County, Illinois. They elected a captain and two lieutenants, determined that the first wagon of one day would be the last wagon of the next, and set off. Every morning they brewed huge pots of sweet coffee, which they drank throughout the day. Every night they staked their oxen, circled their wagons, and fried their bacon. That year the Indians were peaceful, but just behind them the travelers feared epidemics of cholera. They traveled north along the Platte and the North Platte into Wyoming to the Sweetwater River, through the South Pass, across the Continental Divide, into Idaho. At Fort Hall, on the Snake River, the company split, some going south to California, others north, along the Snake, to Oregon. John and his friends headed north; in the Willamette Valley they sold their team and their wagon, bought packhorses, and made their way south into the goldfields between Eureka and Redding in the Shasta and Salmon mountains.

The first day John set up his rocker, searching for bright spots in the gravel of a gulch, he took out $100 worth of gold. Then, for the next three weeks, he took out only enough to pay for his rice and fatback. It was something that happened again and again: the first, heady strike, then weeks of empty washings, and, finally, a restless move to another claim only to hear, a month later, that the man who'd come after them had taken $1,000 a day out of the muddy ditch they'd abandoned. Meanwhile, sutlers grew rich, selling potatoes and onions for $1 apiece. Once, working a claim near the Salmon River, John dug $360 worth of ore out of a crevice with a spoon, a butcher knife, and a pick. Another time, on another claim, he scraped out $400. Once he found a nugget as big as the end of his thumb. All around were Indians who faded in and out of sight, through the trees and ravines, calling to each other like owls, sniping at the miners with old English muskets and stealing their horses. Every miner carried a gun. Sometimes the miners killed deer, sometimes each other, sometimes Indians. Once a small party of Indians stole the horses of John and his friends. For two days the Indians kept just out of gunshot, hooting and making obscene gestures. In 1852 John grew tired of the life. He packed up his gold along with a copy of *Plutarch's Lives* that he had somehow acquired and took a steamer from Portland to San Francisco. From there he traveled to Panama, crossed the Isthmus, and then docked in New Orleans, where he took his ore to a mint and, in his words, "got coin for it." Two weeks later he was back in Griggsville, an adventurer working for his father in the lumber business.

In 1860 he and his father voted for Abraham Lincoln, the man from Springfield, who had said, in public, that he would never abolish slavery, only stop its spread. In 1861, when Lincoln called for 75,000 volunteers, John mustered in for three months. In 1862, when Lincoln called for 300,000 more, John entered the 129th Illinois as a private. In September his regiment was ordered to Louisville, Kentucky, where he was made a commissary captain. Outside Frankfort, Kentucky, he walked across a field covered with dead. Here and there he saw feet and hands sticking out of the ground. His regiment was ordered to Bowling Green, Kentucky, to guard the rail line between Louisville and Nashville, Tennessee. There he was made quartermaster with the rank of lieutenant. He regretted the appointment since his travels across the plains and the hard itinerant life he had lived as a miner made him long to be a scout, out ahead of everyone, taking his chances, learning the truth while others waited.

From Bowling Green, his brigade was ordered to Lookout Mountain, Chattanooga. There he served under a drunk rooster of a man named General Joseph Hooker. In May 1864 his regiment crossed into Georgia. At Resaca he was part of a charge that lasted a few minutes and lost 100 men. From Resaca, under the command of William T. Sherman, his division broke through to Marietta, on the Chattahoochee River. Four miles outside Atlanta he fought in the Battle of Peachtree Creek, where the Confederates of General John Bell Hood were caught in a crossfire. The next day, on an acre of ground, he counted 128 corpses. He went to a field hospital,

searching for one of his sergeants who was said to have been wounded. The surgeons had taken planks from an old mill, set them on trestles, and used them for operating tables. There were trenches dug underneath them. "The surgeons worked like butchers, amputating legs and arms, and throwing them under the tables." When John finally found his sergeant, he saw that the man had lost his leg. "'Cap,' said the sergeant, 'I believe I'm going to go.' And he did." John noted that the officers of his regiment were each drawing half a gallon of whiskey a day from his stores.

At the end of July, Sherman ordered his troops to burn everything they couldn't carry and march to the sea. "My last impression of Atlanta was an immense smoke." John was ordered to forage for supplies and keep his wagons full. He was to feed 3,000 men. He ordered twenty-five infantrymen to scour the countryside. By nightfall they all had returned on horseback. They took sweet potatoes and just-harvested fodder from the fields. They took live hogs and raided smokehouses; at one time he had a herd of 800 cattle. One day his men found $100,000 in Confederate bills at the bottom of a corncrib. From then on, whatever they took, they paid for. After short rations for so long, he said, the march to the sea "was kind of a picnic . . . a regular holiday. . . . I don't suppose there was ever a happier army than Sherman's." In Milledgeville, Georgia, his foragers found a box of freshly printed but unsigned

Confederate currency worth half a million dollars. John gave it to the soldiers of his regiment, who signed the scrip as they pleased. Huge crowds of black women and children followed them everywhere, refusing to leave. Finally, he ordered them to halt on one side of a bridge, and after his men had gone across, he ordered the bridge destroyed. They kept the black men to fell trees and build roads. By the time they passed through Savannah and turned up the coast into South Carolina, Lincoln had been murdered. In June 1865 John mustered out in Washington and returned to Illinois.

In 1883 John's father died. He was, said John, "as true as steel. Dark, quick . . . sociable, and kindhearted," he had prospered in his business and, ten years before his death, had become president of his own bank. John inherited that bank as well as the land his father owned, and by the time his own son, the second John McWilliams, was a young man, the family had grown rich. The first John McWilliams had never attended anything but a one-room schoolhouse, but he sent his son to a fine preparatory school and then on to Princeton. After college the young man returned and, for seven years, served in the family bank as an assistant cashier and the manager of the family's farms.

In 1911 the second John McWilliams did what his father had dreamed of: He went to California and made a fortune. He began by buying land in Bakersfield. By 1926 he owned huge tracts in the San Fernando Valley and two banks in Pasadena. Ten years later, in a corporate partnership, he owned shares of a 20,000-acre fruit, cotton, and cattle farm in the San Joaquin Valley, ranches in Arkansas, and other farms in Tennessee. He served as president of the local Chamber of Commerce and the Red Cross; he endowed and, for forty years, sat on the board of a great hospital; he served as a trustee of Princeton and attended the summer outings of the Bohemian Club.

The same year he'd left his home in Illinois, he met and married Julia Haverhill, the daughter of a man who owned a paper mill in Adams, Massachusetts. The Haverhills had come to Massachusetts in the 1620s. The first one had been shipwrecked, blown ashore, and robbed of his clothes by Indians. Some had settled in Duxbury, north of Plymouth; others, in New Bedford, the port Herman Melville had called an "anthill in the sea" whose sailors were "sea hermits . . . overrun[ning] and conquer-[ing] the watery world like so many Alexanders; parcelling out among them the Atlantic, Pacific, and Indian oceans . . . liv-[ing] on the sea as prairie cocks in the prairie. . . ." Among the Haverhills of Duxbury was one called King Caesar, who built sloops and brigantines and then, in partnership with others, engaged in the Triangular Trade, carrying rum and iron to West Africa, trading it for gold dust, pepper, and slaves, carrying the slaves, in the deadly Middle Passage, to ports in the West

Indies, and bringing back bills of exchange drawn upon Liverpool merchants and sugar and molasses for the distilleries of New England. Among this man's descendants was the daughter of the paper manufacturer. Between 1912 and 1917 she gave birth to one son and two daughters. Her son was the third John McWilliams. Every day, when he was a boy, his mother would call out to him, as he left the house, "Stand up straight! Be somebody!" His father kept his distance. Years later the fourth John McWilliams, the great-grandson of the man who had been the forty-niner, recalled that his grandfather, the owner of banks, farms, and ranches, was more affectionate to him than he was to his own son. By the time his grandson was old enough to remember him, he had become a fine and proper gentleman, whose life was one of tradition, decorum, and ritual carried on with the help of servants in a fine house, graced by formal and English gardens, hidden behind a brick wall. The son of an adventurer, he had become the bulwark of his family, a Victorian gentleman who, his grandson noticed without understanding, often seemed on the verge of ardent tears.

When the third John McWilliams came of age, he applied to Princeton, but for reasons the young man couldn't understand, he was refused admission. He took the refusal as a sign, and although he could have gone to another college, he chose instead to enter the paper company founded by his mother's father. He was a proud young man, uneasy with abstractions but fascinated by the perfect reality of machines. If Princeton would not have him, then he would start at the bottom of a family business and work his way up. He would be somebody, but not of his father's making. He would live a life not of stocks and options but of great calibrated machines that could turn mountains of rags into reams of the finest paper. Instead of hushed conversations conducted in clubs and conference rooms with his peers, he would stand on a factory floor and talk to foremen at the top of his lungs.

Soon after he made his decision to go to work, he proposed marriage to a well-bred young woman whose family moved in the same circles as his own. When she accepted him, he brought her East, and, because she considered it her duty as a wife, she left the urbane amusements and genteel comforts of Los Angeles and settled with him in the small company town of Adams, deep in the mountains of northwestern Massachusetts. In July 1941 she gave birth to her first child, a boy who was named, as his father, his grandfather, and his great-grandfather had been, John McWilliams.

McWilliams was born in the sign of Cancer, the sign of the crab, a watery, emotional sign, ruled by the feminine element of the moon. His first memory was his mother's warmth followed by her sudden absence and then panic and loneliness. At that moment the sight of the ocean filled his eyes. He was her firstborn son; she wanted him to be perfect. Unfortunately he wasn't. She took him to specialists, each with tests more elaborate than the other. They examined his eyes, his teeth, and his posture. In spite of them, his feet and his teeth stuck out, and his eyesight was astigmatic. He was, he said, "a perfect monstrosity." He was too big for his age. He was moody, clumsy, afraid of heights, afraid of dying, afraid of slimy things, afraid of the dark. His father kept his distance and told him to buck up. His mother fretted and nagged. In school his teachers didn't know what to do. He couldn't learn to read, couldn't follow directions, couldn't answer their questions. It was 1948; he had dyslexia, but no one knew it. So every day they sent him out into the hall and told him to paint murals. The other kids stayed away from him. After school he went to reading specialists' offices, where he sat, staring at words and pictures flashing on the walls, whizzing past him with no more effect than a swarm of flies buzzing around the head of a calf.

By the time he was in the fourth grade the school principal called in his parents, cleared his throat, and told them that in his opinion, their son was mentally retarded. They told the principal he was incompetent. There were fine private boarding schools in the area. If the public school didn't know what to do and if, in truth, they didn't either, then they would send their son to a place that could deal with him. Nothing else had worked. They weren't cruel but baffled. They sent him to a school on top of a nearby mountain. There he lay in his cubicle at night, weeping, wanting his mother, swallowing his sobs. He did two things to escape: First, he quickly learned how to read. He read *Beau Geste* and Jack London and science fiction. One weekend, when he was home visiting his parents, he found his grandfather's book and took it back to school with him. He read about the prairies, the Indians, the gold, and the Civil War. It was only natural that the next thing he learned to do was run away, through the gates, down the mountain, along the tracks, into the little towns. Either the druggists would spot him while he was drinking a Coke and call the school, or the teachers would catch him sneaking back. It didn't matter. It was wonderful just to run free.

Four years later his father's career ran into a brick wall: He had become head of production, but he wanted to be president of the company. He may not have wanted to own all the San Fernando Valley, but he thought he could manage things better than his mother's relatives. On paper he and his partners acquired control of the company, and they voted him in as president, but the operation was a family affair that ran on blood, not stockholdings. He maintained himself as president for a time, but the pressures were too great. He sold out and moved back to California. At the age of forty-three he started again, while, at the age of fourteen, his son watched. For a year the boy flew back and forth across the country during school vacations. His father had been entrusted with enough of his own father's wealth not to need a job, but he desperately wanted one. He'd load his family into the car and drive out to look at ranches. He could have bought any of them. He'd stare and stare at the brown hills, thinking and imagining. The boy would stand next to him, full of fantasies. His mother would stay in the car and complain. She'd spent nearly twenty years in the middle of nowhere; she wasn't about to spend the next twenty on a cattle farm or a fruit ranch. His father would blink like a man waking from sleep, then turn back to the car and drive home. Sometimes he'd stay in his workshop, carefully turning a bowl on his lathe while his son watched the spinning circles cut by the chisel, listening to him talk of quality and persistence as the bowl grew deeper. Every vacation, from then until McWilliams went to college, his father would load their boat onto the top of the car, and the two of them would drive into the Sierras, to lakes where no one went, lakes so quiet and deep that every time the boy cast his fly, it wasn't a question of whether a trout would strike but whether it would be the big one by the rock or the enormous one beside it.

When McWilliams was fifteen, his parents sent him to a boarding school near Pikes Peak. Whenever he could, he ran off into the mountains, scared and exhilarated by the adventure. He stayed at the school until one evening in winter, when an older boy bribed a kitchen worker to turn out the lights in the dining hall during supper. Chairs and salt shakers, milk pitchers and sugar bowls flew through the dark. McWilliams crawled under a table. A month later the headmaster resigned, and McWilliams went back to a school in the East. His new school was "a pretty thin place," he said, full of boys who played football while they waited their chance to become "lawyers, salesmen, and undertakers." McWilliams spent his time skipping off campus or painting a sunburst mandala, carefully adding flake after flake of cadmium yellow to its center. He became the campus artist, beatnik, intellectual. He read Zen and Kerouac and talked to his teachers about magic and religion. During the summers he worked in an architect's office.

In his senior year he applied for admission to the Rhode Island School of Design. The school accepted him and, in his words, "saved my life." He spent a year learning basic design and drawing. A third of his class dropped out, but he remained, confident of himself as an artist. The next year he decided to study architecture. There were only two problems: He couldn't stand the thought of working in an office for the rest of his life, and all his designs were returned to him marked "too decorative and fanciful." He began to realize that he was no more fit to be an architect than an undertaker. He walked around, wearing a sports jacket, his socks held up by garters, thinking he had made a terrible mistake.

It was then that he met Ariel and fell in love. She was a Jewess and an artist, the child of one world and the inhabitant of another that paid little attention to the codes of self-denial, reticence, and duty that his mother called perfection and his father called persistence. McWilliams wanted her, and Ariel let him. A year later they decided to marry. Her parents were more appalled than his. McWilliams was happier than he'd ever been. He was sure the marriage would sever his ties with his family "like a knife." By then his parents had returned to live in the East. In the fall of his junior year he hitchhiked to their home and told them his decision to marry was final. Then he walked away, down their long driveway, "in the rain and sleet, crying like a fool," the golden retrievers frisking after him while he shouted at them, "Go back, go back!" A few weeks later he and Ariel were married. His parents attended the wedding and gave the couple a car.

That year he bought a used 35 mm camera to take pictures of architectural sites. A drugstore processed his film. One day he dropped off a roll, bought another, and then went out and immediately shot it. The next day he did the same thing. And the next day as well. It went on for four months. He was astonished. Photography became, he said, "a recognition of myself and the world around me. For the first time, I felt I could take the things of the world and assimilate them, in any kind of order and sense. I couldn't do it in architecture. It didn't make sense to me. Photography was the first time the world ever made sense. It meant everything to me. It was the most beautiful realization I'd ever had in my life. It was so amazing to me." He bought a 35 mm Pentax and talked his way into the darkroom of a local paper as a lab technician. By the summer he was being sent out on assignments. After years of being forced to live by the rules in dormitories, he began to use the camera as an excuse to wander around, "not caring about anything, just *rummaging* around, wandering the streets for a day, just *looking,* making discoveries, throwing myself into an open situation where things bounced off me and I bounced off them." Like a cane or a hearing aid, the camera became a device he used to overcome his reticence, satisfy his curiosity, and realize a vision that, until then, had remained inaccessible and unexpressed because of dyslexia. At the end of the year Ariel gave birth to their first child, a girl, and for the first time he began to feel as if his insides were made of a whole piece. It had been ten years since his school principal had declared him mentally retarded. By accident, he had discovered a machine that first was to teach him to speak and eventually taught him to sing.

He asked to study with Harry Callahan, a man who, for years, had photographed his wife and child as if they were the inhabitants of an empty earth and had then walked the streets of Chicago, photographing the heads, shoulders, and bodies of women, abstracted by wells of deep shadow, sliced by the sun. Callahan sensed the nature of McWilliams's obsession and accepted him in the program. Callahan's assistant was a man named Dick Libowitz, as passionate, skeptical, and politically engaged as Callahan was understated and undemonstrative. The effect of both these men was to send McWilliams into the streets of the nearby mill towns, where he developed a style inspired by both Callahan's Chicago pictures and Libowitz's politics. Three feet from an oncoming passerby, McWilliams would raise the camera to his eye; decide and manually adjust shutter speed, exposure, and composition; and make a photograph long before the subject, often an old woman, had time to register his presence. He became fluid and instinctive. During the same period, he began to use a large-format four- by five-inch view camera, a cumbersome device that had to be positioned on a tripod but that permitted him to view his subject on a large ground glass screen and to correct perspective distortion by adjusting either the angle of the lens or the focal plane of the film. When he wasn't making pictures of dazed old women, he was using his view camera to record the tenement houses and decayed industrial landscape of the region. His senior show, which included examples of both types of images, was so well received that he de-

cided to continue to study with Callahan for a master's degree.

As an undergraduate McWilliams had not had to compete for Callahan's attention. He was, he said, "the golden boy" of the department. But when he returned as a graduate student, he discovered a young man named Emmett Gowan ready to take his place. The two of them were so much the same but so different that they formed a friendship salted with the rivalry of brothers. Gowan was southern; McWilliams, northern. Gowan had married a fundamentalist Christian; McWilliams, a Jewess. Gowan, inspired by Callahan, chose to photograph his family as if they inhabited an Eden after the Fall. McWilliams, also inspired by Callahan, had gone spinning out into the streets. The result of this rivalry was that when things went well for McWilliams, he loved Callahan as if he were a father; when things went against him, he became "belligerent, rebellious, and antagonistic," like a neglected child.

Callahan did his best to ignore the rivalry and deflect the projections. Perhaps once or twice a month he would invite his graduate students to come to his house for a critique. The contents of a photographic critique, an occasion for the display of new work, can range from a silent nod and a simple question about paper surface to a brief discussion of formalist concerns to a series of accusations, denials, and confessions based upon manifest and latent content. The critiques in which Callahan and his students participated had as much to do with motive as method; they lasted until they ran out of alcohol and everyone went home. One night, or perhaps one morning, somewhere in the middle or maybe at the end of one of these encounters, Callahan excused himself and returned with boxes and boxes of his own contact sheets. As McWilliams was to say years later, "Harry revealed his process." What he revealed were hundreds and hundreds of pictures, some resolved, some unresolved; some clear, others obscure; some foolish and some wise. The master did not simply show his students his feet of clay. He showed them his path, how it meandered, paused, straightened, strayed, stopped, and then collided with what he was satisfied to call his art. In *Zen in the Art of Archery,* a German named Eugen Herrigel journeyed to the East to study Zen archery. After four years he occasionally hit the target, but even when he did, his master would grow impatient and then angry with him. One day Herrigel devised a shooting method and scored a hit. The next day his master refused even to speak with him. After Herrigel had recovered, his master said, "You see what comes of not being able to wait without purpose in a state of highest tension? You cannot even learn to do this without continually asking yourself: Shall I be able to manage it? Wait patiently and see what comes and how it comes!" Herrigel said he'd already waited four years; he was running out of time. The master said it didn't matter; the important

thing was for the shot to fall from the archer like snow from an overburdened leaf. Before he could hit the target, he had to arrive at that state of tension when what happens *must* happen. The night when Callahan brought out his contact sheets and showed them to his students, he revealed the necessity of their wandering to that point where pictures breed pictures, where the very process breeds its fruition.

McWilliams found that process for himself on the sea. In his last year as an undergraduate and more and more often during the two years that followed, he began to sail out from Providence in a twenty-foot boat, into Narragansett Bay and, beyond that, into Rhode Island Sound. For three years he gave himself to the wind and the water, as if he were both a kite and the man who held the string. To get from port to destination and return involved a series of oblique compromises, of tacks and jibes, of good and bad fortune that brought him to a series of points, unpredictable and ephemeral, until the moment he passed through them on the way to his goal, like a man climbing a ladder whose next rung remains invisible until he reaches for it. At the same time that he was sailing out beyond the land, he was making photographs that were smaller in scale and more self-conscious and controlled than the expansive pictures of exploration and appropriation he had made as an undergraduate. Perhaps because of Callahan's simple, insistent questioning of motives, perhaps because of the challenge posed by Gowan's revelatory pictures of his own family, McWilliams began to make nude photographs of Ariel as well as of other women, and for the first time he began to make photographs of nature, "all things," he said, "equated with my own emotions; all senses of my own sexuality." Out of this scrutiny and the constrained photographs it bred came evidence of his own appetites, appetites for other women and for a world beyond Ariel, who, by then, was more deeply in love with their baby than with him. It was, he said, "a very painful, inward, self-evaluating time."

In due course, RISD awarded him a master's degree, shook his hand, and out into the world he went, full of more questions about himself, his desires, intentions, and abilities than ever. First, he tried commercial work, but it didn't last. Then he tried architectural photography, but he grew bored. Finally, he found a job as a photography instructor in New York and began a commute that lasted a year. Sometime in the middle of it, stranded on the tracks between New Haven and Manhattan, he closed his eyes and was engulfed by a voyaging fantasy. There he was, a solitary sailor, crossing the oceans alone, sailing single-handedly around the globe, totally self-sufficient, a hero, without need of the love of women. As soon as the train pulled into Grand Central, he went to a store and bought an armful of books about ocean sailing and circumnavigation. By the end of the year he had scoured every bookstore in the city, rooting out obscure printings, journals, and accounts of single-handed ocean voyages. He accumulated hundreds of volumes. Now, in his fantasies, he built his own hull, launched it, and then lived through a whole voyage, battling the elements with skill and strength until, finally, he came into port, greeted by crowds calling out their love, support, and recognition. A year out of school he returned to Providence and took a job in a Portuguese boatyard. When he was young, he had watched his father work with tools; as he'd grown older, he'd learned to use them himself and to persist until the work was done. Everyone else in the boatyard spoke Portuguese, but it didn't matter. His father had taught him well; he was eager and so inexperienced that the owners could pay him what they wanted and still consider it a favor. He worked for them as a carpenter, not building the hulls but finishing them, building bulkheads, structural supports, cabinets, and decking, changing the configurations, depending on whether the sixteen-footers were to become launches, yacht tenders, or fishing boats. In a year, he finished eighteen, working alone in a shed whose doors opened onto the expanse of the sound.

That year he bought an enormous, derelict old house, moved his family in, and began to restore it. It may have been the gentility of its architecture and its sheer size, or it may have been the cold and gloom of the winter, or it may have been the daily round of early-to-bed, early-to-rise imposed by a young family and a job—whatever it was, he began to feel as if he were trapped again on the top of a mountain. It had been nearly twenty years since he'd been sent away from home to sleep in a cubicle.

This time he escaped in a car, headed south. He went with a friend from graduate school, a fellow named Jim Dow who, like an innocent middle brother, had escaped the rivalry between Gowan and McWilliams. Once Dow had asked McWilliams if he had ever heard of a photographer named Walter Evans, and McWilliams had told him the artist's first name was Walker. Informed of that, Dow began a study of Evans that had consumed him until, three years later, he and McWilliams were on their way into the South, trading Agee and Evans anecdotes, growing more and more excited by the prospect of seeing the region that had inspired *Let Us Now Praise Famous Men*. On their first day they reached Virginia. After the cold, stale dead ends of New England, it seemed as if they'd opened a door to a fresh and fragrant garden. It was, said McWilliams, "like a *dream!* Just passin' through the countryside. High all the time. On the trip. On the differences. The desolation. The mystery. The small towns. The Mississippi River. The way the land was. The way the buildings were. The things going by in the car—the road kill, the signs. All those things I'd never seen before. All the things I felt in myself. In places where I could feel the rhythms and power of things. Even be able to make some sense out of it." From Virginia they traveled into the Smokies and paused there, in the sun, above the clouds.

Then they crossed into Alabama. It was soon after the voting rights march in Selma, and they were driving a car with Massachusetts plates. Dow told a story he'd heard about Alabama, an Indian legend about the daughter of a chief, raped by white trappers, and how the chief had called down a curse on the land and how the stars had fallen on it and scorched it and filled it with deformed and malignant people. They headed for Selma. On their way through a small town McWilliams spotted an old shack he wanted to photograph. Sitting alone in front of it was a retarded boy who barely nodded when McWilliams asked permission to take a picture. By the time he set up his tripod, men from a lumberyard down the road had spotted them. One of them had a gun. "You boys better get off and outta here. We gonna call the *law!*" they said. Dow and McWilliams got back in their car, "shaking in our shoes," McWilliams said, frightened that even as they drove away, they'd be run off the road and beaten. But when time passed and nothing happened, they grew more and more exhilarated.

By evening they had reached another little town and walked into its old hotel to get something to eat. On the menu, at the bottom, beneath the side orders of greens and black-eyed peas and navy beans, was something they'd never heard of, something called chess pie. Was it, they wondered, something less elaborate than a checker tart, something with squares, served with rooks? When the waitress came, they asked. "Chess Pyhe?!" she said. "You must be northern boys!" Then, after a long explanation of how she used only fresh eggs in hers, and after she had brought their chicken and gravy and yellow squash and yams and collards and peas and cabbage, she returned with two big slices of chess pie. "Dessert's on the house," she said.

Finally they reached Selma, parked their car, and, dressed in coats and ties, crossed the very bridge the marchers had crossed, feeling as if every eye were on them, excited by the history and drama they had touched and by the chances they believed they had taken to be there. It was, said McWilliams, "a very romantic undertaking. All I remember is that when I got back to Providence, I wanted to leave, real bad."

He returned to find a letter waiting for him from a second-rate state university in Atlanta, offering him a teaching job. He'd always believed in his own timing; he'd always considered it a born gift, like the ability of others to win races and to sing. The only thing he knew about Atlanta was that his great-grandfather had had a hand in burning it, but even that precedent was a good omen, set out like a beacon. The university said it wanted him to build a program in photography. McWilliams put on a suit and flew down for an interview. At the end of the day he was brought for inspection before the school's president, a 285-pound former defensive lineman who came booming out of his office, ignored McWilliams's hand, faked a knee kick, and then grabbed him in a bear hug, while he asked in a stage whisper, "You aren't a Communist or a homosexual, are you, boy?" McWilliams said no, and he had the job.

The city he'd fallen into had been run for years by a coalition of white businessmen whose idea of progress was to make themselves as attractive as possible to northern investors. One result was a city used as a regional outpost by the Fortune 500, where young, prospective upper-middle managers spent a few years, competing with one another for market share while the guys upstairs kept track of their performances and occasionally thinned the litter. Another result was that the local business elite was full of good old boys who had somehow managed only to bend the law while accumulating a few banks in counties whose principal industries were either carpet mills or chicken farms. Since both the locals and their northern patrons preferred a business climate based on racial avoidance rather than violence, when a would-be governor like Lester Maddox reached for an ax handle to defend his restaurant, and when organizations like the SCLC, SNCC, and CORE mounted demonstrations, orchestrated by men in such

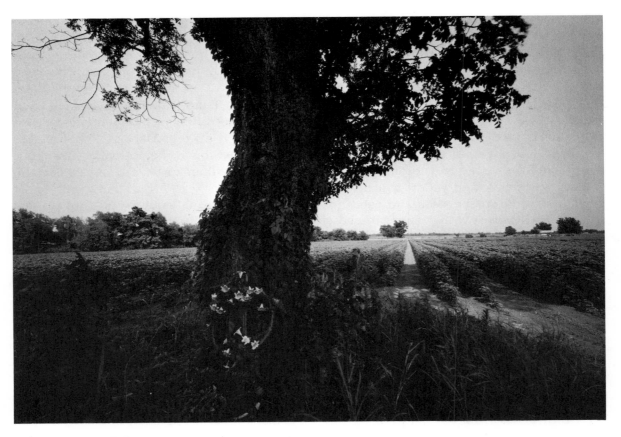

SOYBEANS, ARKANSAS, 1977

jeopardy that from one moment to the next they didn't know if they were going to be in church, jail, or the morgue, the city's business elite responded with a policy of opportunistic compromise and reconciliation based on the slogan "A City Too Busy to Hate."

Whatever patrons of the arts there had been had nearly all been killed when their chartered jet had crashed outside Paris in 1962. In their memory the survivors had built a memorial arts center whose chief virtue was that it existed where none had been before but that looked as if it were part of a franchise run by the same company that owned the Lincoln and Kennedy centers. The city itself had begun life in the 1840's as a rail depot called Terminus, and because of Sherman's efforts, it had no significant architectural structures built before the 1880's. Its principal university ran on soft-drink money; its fine arts radio station presented the news each morning by reading aloud the daily paper, including the comics, and copies of *The New York Times* were as rare and unavailable as those of the *London Illustrated News* or the *Frankfurter Allgemeine Zeitung*. Although there were a few Italian and Chinese restaurants, there was no cuisine. Cooking was often modified with the word "home," and what delicatessens there were sometimes served chopped liver on white bread with mayonnaise.

In spite of these shortcomings, the city had been blessed by nature. Its skies were as clear, blue, and bottomless as lakes, swept clean by winds that blew high, dense cumulus clouds across it, 1,000 feet above sea level. Everywhere there were trees: pines and hickories, water oaks and sweet gums, dogwoods, redbuds, and magnolias. Atlanta's springs were so redolent, their colors so hallucinatory, its falls so pungent that it seemed as if the seasons themselves had been invented in the region and then exported to the North. Roses bloomed into October; azaleas came in April and lasted till June; crepe myrtles flamed scarlet in July. In summer, in the afternoons, thunderstorms flushed the streets and left them steaming. Businessmen and their wives survived inside, protected by air conditioning and insecticides, while outside, at the edge of neighborhoods, black vendors sold ribs, barbecued on grills made of fifty-gallon oil drums, sliced lengthwise and propped up on their sides. Everywhere, over everything, growing a foot a day, crawled kudzu vines, their purple flowers smelling like grape soda, their leaves and tendrils covering trees, streets, walks, signs, houses, and buildings, encompassing everything beneath an endless green undulant wave.

Into this landlocked sea of trees, flowers, and vines McWilliams drove with his family, dragging behind him an old Scandinavian sloop he had bought in Baltimore. He intended to restore it, haul it to Savannah, and then sail away. Instead, he pushed off into the depths of his own mind and ambitions. Nearly as soon as he arrived in Atlanta, he felt as if he were in a place "that wasn't at all connected to my past," a place "of tremendous freedom, freedom to *shape,* to do anything I wanted to do."

McWilliams temporarily forgot the inevitabilities of his own soul. One of the agents of this forgetfulness was marijuana. At the time of his arrival Atlanta may have been without fine restaurants, but it was an important regional black market for some of the finest marijuana smuggled in from Jamaica, Mexico, and Colombia. Like the fruits and vegetables of an itinerant peddler, much of the most potent marijuana that then entered the United States through Florida and Georgia either had been picked over or had already been sold by the time it reached the North. As a student McWilliams had smoked a few joints, but nothing as potent or as plentiful as the dope that moved from hand to hand in Atlanta. Used, if not as a sacrament, then as a means to remember, delight in, and pay homage to the obvious, the marijuana bred a humor, spontaneity, and candor that allowed those who smoked it to forgive themselves and others for their appetites and to recognize the difference between imposed conventions and instinctive feelings.

Freed, for the moment, of his past, McWilliams began to make photographs in his own backyard that had none of the constraints of the pictures he had made as a graduate student. An unfocused, ethereal nude, her legs spread apart and her head thrown back, floated just above the ground. A young man, draped in a sheet spread to reveal his genitals, sat half in and half out of the sun, his bearded face hidden in the leaves and branches of an azalea hedge that cast shadows, like floral tattoos, across the skin of his arms and shoulders. McWilliams's daughter, a beautiful child of seven years with the astounding face of a Pre-Raphaelite heroine, sat on a kitchen chair, against a background of morning glory and tomato vines, her legs apart, her dress pulled up to her throat, revealing the cotton panties and torso of a little girl, but the legs and thighs of a young woman. Again and again he photographed his child, sometimes as part of a tableau of growth and fruition, sometimes as the figure in a play of incestuous desire. Once he photographed her sitting in front of the giant leaves of an elephant-ear plant, holding on her lap a painting so large that it hid all but her head, thighs, and legs—a painting of a tropical landscape at whose center was an hourglass-shaped fjord that mimicked the sensual curves of a woman's body. Another time he photographed her with his view camera, fitted with a wide-angle lens that allowed light to strike only the center of the film, creating a dark, circular vignette around the edges of the finished print, at whose center she stood with

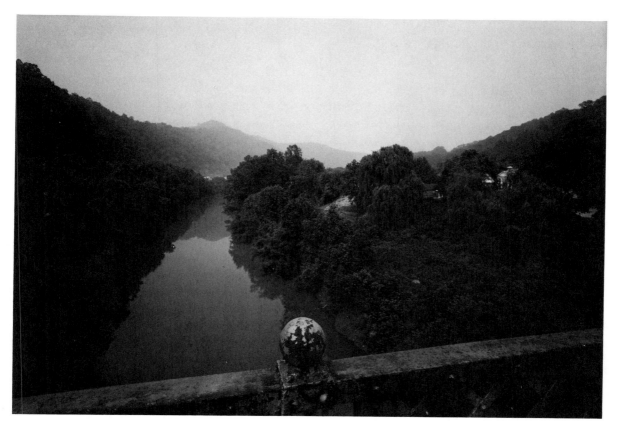

EASTERN KENTUCKY, 1977

her head back and her hands clasped, as if she had been interrupted in prayer, while behind her the strands of a dense grove of bamboo shot up out of the ground into the air, higher than the rooftops, like the feathered spray of a fountain. In a series of pictures he made with an eight- by ten-inch camera set on a tripod, activated by a bulb release, he photographed himself holding her on his lap, his hands around her belly, her hands dangling between her thighs, a look of sly contentment on her face while, in the background, in the leafless branches of a bush, two jump ropes hung like tree snakes coiled in Eden. Once he even photographed her holding a skull in her lap, looking up at him with heavy-lidded indifference, as if she were Salome and he, poor man, were John the Baptist, gazing at the reward of his own temptation.

At the same time that he was making what he called his garden pictures, he began to explore the countryside, first through the acquaintance of a young woman, "*very* southern, very aristocratic-looking," whom he photographed in the overgrown formal gardens of a decrepit plantation, and then in the company of some of his own students. As their teacher he demanded the openness and granted a freedom that was rarely found in families and very seldom found in schools. As much as he demanded, he gave, and as much as he gave, he asked to be given. In exchange for sharing the lessons he had painfully learned from Callahan, he asked first one, then another, and then another of the young men who were his students to guide him to places and people he had never known and to love him like a brother.

Over the years he established such bonds with three of his students. The first two showed him the land and its people. The third taught him more than he needed to know about the city and its politics. The first of his brotherly guides was a young man who worked in the display department of a local store. In the course of his work McWilliams's student had met many homosexuals, and although he himself was a lover of women rather than men, he had grown familiar with the homosexual bars and clubs of both Atlanta and Savannah. Together he and McWilliams traveled to Savannah, and after McWilliams had spent the day photographing the squares, fountains, façades, and graveyards of the city, his student introduced him to a gay world that he had never seen. A year later McWilliams was to meet another student, in whose company he traveled to South Carolina. His second guide had spent years studying the Gullah-speaking blacks who lived on the Sea Islands off the coast, near Charleston. Although McWilliams had once lived in a neighborhood in Providence shared by both blacks and whites, he had known few of his black neighbors and considered the few with whom he even talked to be displaced and disoriented failures. He discovered in South Carolina that unlike the blacks he had known in the North,

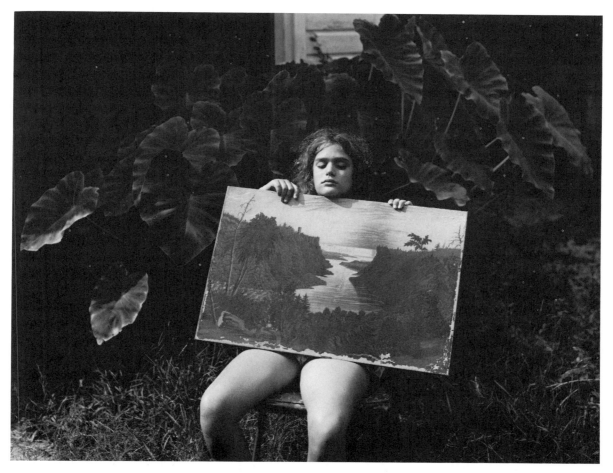

CHARLESTON, SOUTH CAROLINA, 1973

those to whom he was introduced by his student had never left the land; they had, he said, "a very strong identity, a very strong culture; they were a very beautiful, charismatic people." McWilliams and his student went shrimping with them, throwing their nets into creeks. That summer he explored the South Carolina coast, "a wild place, very hot and sultry; steamy, very erotic." At the end of it he photographed his student standing naked in an outdoor shower on the dock of a salt marsh, bounded by a shore of live oaks and pines, the shower head hovering in the air above him, while the water washed away his face, changing him into a figure in a fountain.

In the fall of 1972, three years after his arrival in Atlanta, McWilliams was invited by a committee of patrons, administrators, curators, collectors, and dilettantes to organize the city's yearly Arts Festival, annually held in a park that had originally been the grounds of an International Cotton Exposition organized in the 1880's to attract northern and European investment to the New South. For years the festival had been a modest affair, with a central pavilion haphazardly hung with paintings of tobacco barns juxtaposed with local versions of abstract expressionism and photorealism, interspersed with photographs of sunsets next to displays of earthenware teapots and coffee tables made of whole tree trunks. Outside, families strolled, buying hot dogs, macramé hangings, and glass paperweights, while others listened to fiddlers play country music or watched potters build vases on their wheels. In recent years the smell of marijuana and the sight of young hippies and their dogs had been added to the fair. McWilliams decided that a new opportunity "was being put in my path." He cleared out the mélange in the central pavilion, refinished the walls, and carefully hung them with nothing but photographs—photographs not of sea gulls and children but images that alluded to the work of such modern masters as Jerry Uelsmann, Minor White, Arthur Siegel, and Harry Callahan. Among these photographs he included nudes made by his students as well as his own garden pictures. "Everything," he said, "was being pushed my way to take advantage of it. And I did. Avidly. I featured photography."

Instead of inviting potters to entertain the crowd with the sight of clay being turned into bowls, he invited the photographer Frederick Sommer, the same man who had filled Bill Burke with doubts about "BEAU—TY," to judge the exhibition and hold a workshop open to interested members of the public. Sommer's thinking had had a profound effect on Emmett Gowan, McWilliams's graduate school rival. Gowan believed Sommer to be a savant. McWilliams considered him merely "an interesting old man" who cast himself as a sage. McWilliams met him at the airport in the middle of a rainstorm and took him to the festival pavilion. Sommer had with him a little book of his own writings, page after page of maxims, aphorisms, and paradoxical riddles. A small crowd gathered around him, listening to him read his epigrams and then elaborate on them while the rain fell so heavily that it was difficult to hear what he said. After the reading Sommer reviewed the work displayed in the pavilion and gave awards to several of the nudes. Within a few days there was an uproar: Letters and reviews in the daily papers complained of the exhibition's "pornography"; disgruntled painters and craftspeople reinvented the nineteenth-century debate over photography as a fine art. McWilliams was delighted: The director of the art museum suddenly noticed that there were no contemporary photographers represented in the museum's collection and asked McWilliams's advice. In one well-timed, well-coordinated move, McWilliams had made an entire city conscious of himself and his medium. "Everything was raw," he said. "You could step into any opportunity. . . . I got into the politics of the arts. . . . I was the person with the most energy. I realized I could swing a lot of people. Every institution was naïve. I took the city by storm."

His only problem was that he was employed by a public university, supported and administered by people who went to church every Sunday. McWilliams and his students could get away with showing pictures of women with their dresses up over their heads and men wearing no under-

wear at the Arts Festival, but every time they tried it at the university, the dean or the president ordered the doors of the student gallery locked and the exhibition dismantled. The war in Vietnam had also upset everyone. One of McWilliams's students had been allotted a small alcove space in which to present a coherent statement of his work in a design course. The young man decided to paint the space white, and then, dipping his brush in a jar of blood, he wrote, in large letters, on the wall, "My Country, 'Tis of Thee." Two days later the blood began to stink, and McWilliams's dean, the department chairman, and the former defensive lineman who ran the university told the student to clean up the mess.

For three years McWilliams had taught his students with intensity, humor, candor, and commitment. Every week he had invited them to his house to show and discuss their work and their reasons behind it, just as Callahan had done in Providence. One night, after one of these critiques, several of McWilliams's students—including a young man who was to be McWilliams's third guide—decided that if others could form their own cooperative groceries, health clinics, day care centers, and newspapers, then they could form their own cooperative gallery. There they would be able to show whatever work they believed important or pleasing without the problems they had experienced at the university. In late 1973 they rented a storefront, refurbished it, named it Nexus, and hung their first show. Next door to them was a dance company that had been run out of another local university when its director was accused of practicing witchcraft.

The more active McWilliams became as a spokesman, teacher, and organizer in the city's photography and art community, and the more power he realized he had to effect social change on behalf of his medium, the more involved he became with his own work. He began to travel into the mountains of northern Georgia during the winter, looking for "magical places." At sunset, he said, "I'd either end up in a graveyard in Rome, Georgia, up on top of a hill, or I'd end up on the Etowah Indian mounds," the burial mounds of a pre-Columbian culture, fifty miles from Atlanta. Sometimes he'd watch the sun set in a graveyard in Macon; other times he'd return to photograph the statuary of Bonaventure Cemetery near Savannah. Again and again he'd return to "the eroded landscapes, the moonscapes," and refuse piles of kaolin mines near the very center of the state. "I fell in love with that," he said, "the mounds, the piles, the desolation, the holes, the shit."

Wherever he traveled, he saw land that was "barren, burnt-out, desolate, washed-out, hazed-out. Stretches of pines and nondescript land that looked like it had been there for centuries without change. I felt I had to go under the surface of it. Somewhere, underneath, there were shadows. I

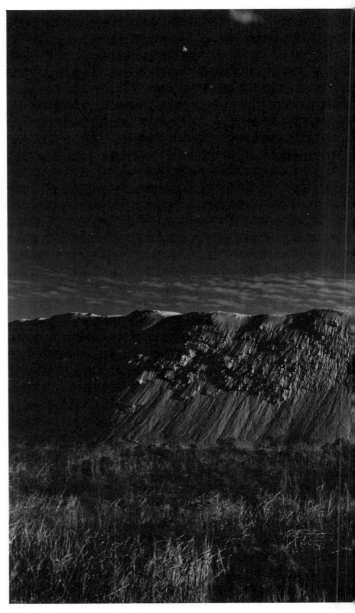

SAND MOUND, FLORIDA, 1977

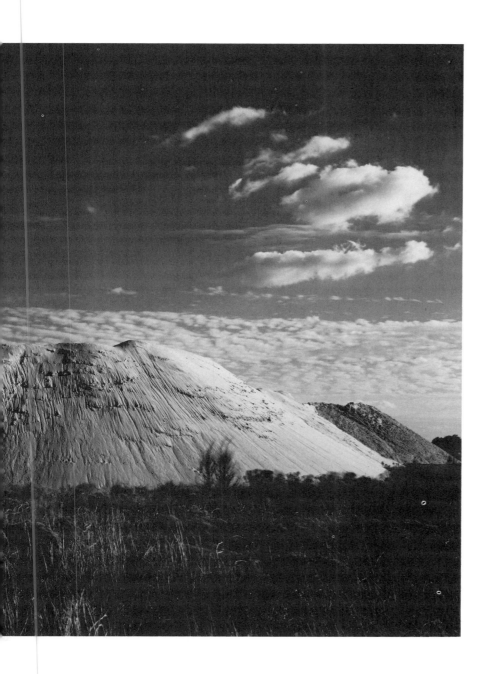

played into what happened in the shadows. The mystery. Gray-dark. Deep-dark. I didn't know what it was—the burnt-out, wild, kudzu-draped landscape. The kudzu in the winter, the long, twisty vine shapes." He took picture after picture of bridges, buildings, and houses twined in the undertow of that vegetable tide, of runneled sand piles that looked as high as Everest and as stark as the Pyramids, and of marble angels encircled by myrtle.

One afternoon he had a vision: "I was standing out underneath a highway bridge. It was twilight. There was an amazing golden light there. I got a sense of the scarred land, the dirt, lit by this prophetic, holy light. It was timeless underneath there. I saw the land for the first time. I looked and saw how it had been shaped to receive the bridge. I saw the stripped land in a golden light. This holy, living, vibrant *light* had changed the space. I could see it was open, malleable, without form, ready to receive whatever structure there was. It was grand. Very grand. But no one had paid any attention. Everyone looked at what was on top, but underneath was the enigma on which everything rested. I'd seen a strange subterranean vista, opening into the light—a vista no one else had seen." What he'd seen down there was the past, holding up the underside of the present, which itself was the underside of the future. Everyone else saw bridge embankments as scars and the refuse piles of mines as garbage heaps left by indiscriminate av-

arice. For most people of McWilliams's age, education, and sensibility, the New South was nothing but a chain of used-car lots built on the edge of strip mines. McWilliams saw it all as an enigmatic prophecy, from which a new human aesthetic would emerge. He knew that people were buried in graveyards, but he also believed that they were places where "the inhabitants manifested themselves poetically." He said: "I began to believe that things would go on and on and on. That man would persevere. That we shaped everything in our own image. That, whatever it was, it was inevitable. Man was nature. I wasn't trying to glorify the situation. There was a lot of neglect and disregard for the future in what we did. But it was still how we manifested our spirit. I was just *seeing* it. I thought I was a prophet seeing signs." He decided, if he could, to become a traveler, recording the past and the future, the hope and the indictment that all were hidden in the shape of the southern land.

Meanwhile, his marriage was ending. He and Ariel had decided to have another child, but the very summer that his son was conceived was the same summer he spent traveling the coast of South Carolina. The same restless curiosity that had made his great-grandfather long to be an army scout; the same discontent that had made his ancestor believe, when he was seventeen, that he had to leave home or die, and that had made him, at fourteen, "crazy to go back to the farm" and to work, for

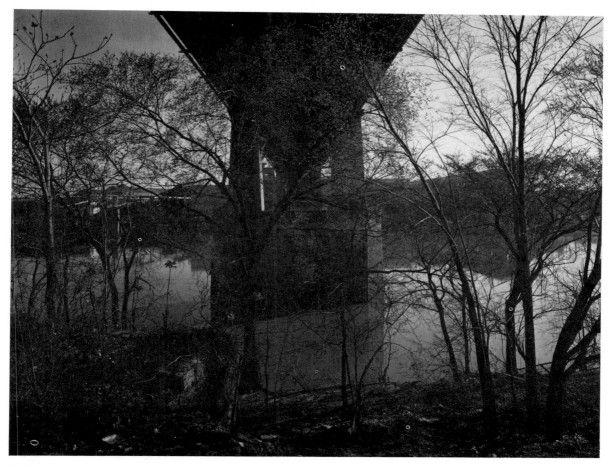

OHIO RIVER, KENTUCKY, 1975

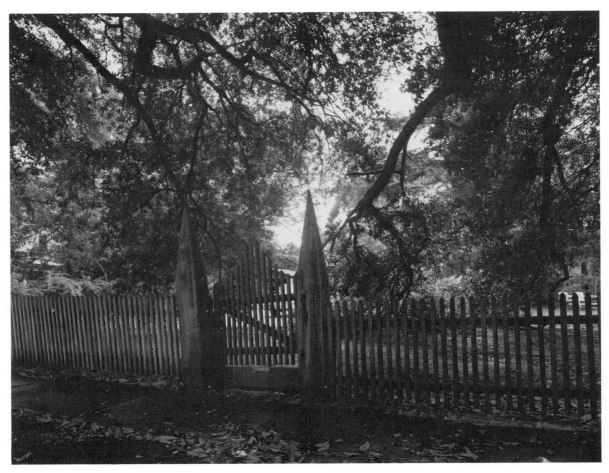

BAMBERG, SOUTH CAROLINA, 1974

months, breaking the raw prairie with an ox team, the same uneasy, restless, curious, nearly physical need simply to go, simply to leave, sucked McWilliams out of his marriage and down the road, just as, long ago, it had sent him running through the gates of the boarding schools.

About the time McWilliams began to grow restless, one of his students began to tunnel his way into the politics of the city of Atlanta. Within a few years the young man had dug a tunnel big enough to stand in and had invited his friends and even his teacher to join him. When, some years later, the roof collapsed, the disaster took part of McWilliams with it. The story of how the tunnel was built and how McWilliams ended up in it began in 1974, when Maynard Jackson became the first black mayor of Atlanta. Jackson had benefited from leadership connections within the Atlanta black community he had inherited from his patrician grandfather, who had insisted that French be spoken in his parlor, and from his father, who had been a Baptist minister, as well as from his education at Morehouse, a prestigious private black college whose graduates referred to Harvard as the Morehouse of the North. Jackson had been elected by a majority of black votes as well as by a modest number of white votes, cast by those who would have described themselves as liberals. To maintain his connections to this politically active, educated, and moneyed white constituency, Jackson had established, within

his administration, a Bureau of International and Cultural Affairs whose policy, if not exactly one of bread and circuses, was designed to improve the quality of the city's cultural life by fostering the arts and by publicizing the mayor's own enlightened efforts. The bureau was directed by another Morehouse graduate known to his friends as the Black Prince, who, until Jackson's election, had passed his time studying Spenser's *Faerie Queene* for a Ph.D. in Elizabethan literature. One of the first things the Black Prince did was to staff the bureau with artists.

Among them was a photographer named Stewart, whose responsibilities were to record such events as the arrival of the Nigerian head of state when he stopped in the city to pay his respects. Two years before Stewart was hired by the bureau, he had been one of McWilliams's best students. It had been Stewart, along with a few others, who had hit upon the idea of a cooperative photographic gallery, and after a few years as the bureau's staff photographer, it was Stewart who learned of an immense but abandoned old school building that the city's Board of Education was anxious to lease to a nonprofit organization. Stewart convinced the board to lease the building to the Nexus Gallery, and then, for two years, he worked day and night to make the building habitable and to convince artists and arts organizations to lease space in it. By 1977, a year after a former governor of Georgia was elected President of the United

States, and two years after McWilliams had found himself standing under a highway bridge, encompassed by a golden light, the former school building was inhabited by such an assortment of painters, sculptors, weavers, potters, photographers, foundry workers, printers, dancers, and opera singers that to walk down one of its corridors was like strolling through the set of the Beatles' film *Yellow Submarine.*

McWilliams took a direct part in the venture. He did everything from sweeping the floors to sitting on the gallery's board of directors. Stewart loved him like an older brother, and constantly confided in him. Together they talked, dreamed, and planned. "Stewart was like fire," McWilliams said, "and I was like water. There was a lot of power in that combination. Together we moved into the politics of art in Atlanta. We'd been given the go-ahead by something or somebody in the city. Everything was falling into place."

Everything except McWilliams's job and his marriage. As much to console herself during McWilliams's absences as to affirm her own sense of worth, Ariel had begun to dance, first as a student and then as a member of the company of dancers whose director had once been accused of witchcraft. The care of her children and the rigors of the constant rehearsals, as well as the powerful, exclusively feminine warmth of the company itself, consumed Ariel, and as McWilliams turned more and more toward the land and its secrets, she turned more and more away from him, toward her own destiny as part of an ensemble of women artists.

Meanwhile, the university where McWilliams taught continued to close exhibitions of his students' work. He argued on behalf of the free expression of a free vision, but he discovered that his chairman had lost patience with him. Every day they argued over something, and every day the man's challenge was "If you don't like it here, why don't you leave?" Even though McWilliams's students admired him and his colleagues respected him, he knew he had as much chance of getting tenure as of crossing the ocean in a rowboat.

In the spring of 1975 he put his best prints in a box and sent them off to the National Endowment for the Arts in Washington. If Jimmy Carter could run for the presidency, he reasoned, why not see what the arts endowment thought of his pictures of kudzu and kaolin mounds and of little girls holding skulls and tropical landscapes in their laps? Soon after he applied to the Endowment, he also applied to the Guggenheim Foundation. He chose the words in his proposal very carefully: In the South, he said, there lived human beings who believed in the principle of unlimited growth. They were in the process of moving mountains and changing the course of rivers. Some sort of prophecy about human fate and human hope was hidden in their indiscriminate scarring of the land. Whatever the prophecy, he said, he wanted to record its marks and their meanings with his camera. At Christmastime the National Endowment awarded him a major grant. Four months later the Guggenheim did the same. Jimmy Carter was sitting with a frozen grin in the White House, and McWilliams had more money and more prestige than people like his chairman knew what to do with. "At the university," he said, "I went from being the horse's ass to the golden boy. . . . I went from shit to being one of the people who was going to give the place some legitimacy." His chairman said he could go if he wanted, but his job might not be there when he came back. Ariel said the same thing about their marriage. McWilliams headed for the door.

The first thing he did was buy an orange truck with four-wheel drive. The next thing he did was ask a sign painter to paint a large fish on the door of the driver's side. Without the fish, the truck looked like part of a state highway department motor pool; with it, it looked like the vehicle of a slightly mad fish and game inspector. "To this day," he said, "I don't know why I had the fish painted there. I knew I wanted *something*, and the fish—I felt as if I was going to swim through a sea of some sort. The fish was my symbol of mobility. And it was a religious symbol. Not necessarily Christian. But I was religious about my work. I talked about prophecies in the land. I was going to preach a gospel."

Over the years he had slowly assembled the technical means to realize his vision. He called it his optical system. Just before he left New England, he had bought a huge old Eastman Autofocus enlarger, a mammoth contraption that in the early twentieth century had been used by a portrait studio in Boston to enlarge eight- by ten-inch glass and nitrate film negatives. McWilliams had hauled the thing South with him along with the Scandinavian sloop he intended to restore. The sloop he'd sold, but the enlarger he had rebuilt and rewired. He had replaced its single tungsten bulb, whose light had illuminated a negative only after passing through condenser lenses, with a set of miniature fluorescent tubes, called a cold head, that sat directly above the negative and illuminated it evenly. Before he refitted the enlarger, its condensers had focused its single yellow light in such a way that the negative image it projected for enlargement was brighter in the center than at the edges, so the print it produced was, without his intervention, always darker in the middle than at its borders. The set of fluorescent tubes he installed produced a diffuse blue-white light that evenly rendered a low contrast print with distinct shadow details—details found in those areas of the negative that appeared nearly transparent but that contained faint traces of graphic information, composed, like the rest of the negative, of patterns made of grains of metallic silver.

To create these patterns, McWilliams used a German view camera, called a Deardorff, that accepted five- by seven-inch sheets of film and could be fitted with a variety of lenses: a 90 mm Super Angula, a very wide-angle lens of superior optical quality; a 150 mm Symmar, also a wide-angle lens; a 203 mm lens, whose field of view approximated that of human vision; and a fourteen-inch semitelephoto lens. With these lenses he used a variety of filters to darken the sky in contrast with the ground or to increase the contrast between the sky and its clouds. He used a red filter if, in the final print, he wished to darken the sky completely; an orange one if he wanted less contrast; and a yellow filter, which he used most often, to increase slightly the difference between sky and clouds and sky and earth. He used a relatively fine-grain black-and-white Kodak film, whose proposed development time he entered next to the number of the film in a log immediately after he had made an exposure.

McWilliams's method of interrelated exposure and development was that of the zone system, originally propagated forty years ago by the master landscape photographer Ansel Adams. Every exposure and every calculation of mutually dependent lens setting and shutter speed were based on light readings made in the shadows of whatever scene McWilliams photographed. If the contrast between elements of the scene was normal, he noted in his log a normal development time with the letter N. But if the day was very clear and bright, if there were great differences between shadows and highlights, then McWilliams wrote, next to the sheet film number in his log, the notation "N − 1," which reminded him to decrease the film's development time by perhaps one-third or one-fourth (depending on the temperature of his chemicals) and so to decrease the contrast between shadows and highlights in the resulting negative. If, however, when he made his original exposure, the day was cloudy and the light flat, he wrote in his log the code "N + 1," which prompted him to increase his development time by an appropriate amount and so increase the contrast of the final negative. In every case he inspected the negative as he developed it, examining crucial highlight detail against a green light which had no effect on the film. In his two years of travel he repeated this process of exposure, notation, and development by inspection 5,000 times. The sixteen- by twenty-inch prints he eventually made from his negatives had a brilliance, a luminous clarity, and a tonal richness of greater sensual impact than the original scenes themselves.

For the first eighteen months of the project he traveled; for the last six he shut himself in his darkroom and did nothing but print. Every two or three weeks during his travels he returned to Atlanta just long enough to develop his negatives, see his children, and register the chaos that was replacing his marriage. By the middle of the project he had moved out of his house and fallen in love with a woman whose face he had once seen in a photograph made by one of his students. Even though he hadn't met the woman at the time, he felt when he saw her portrait as if he'd known her and would know her again, as if the picture had reminded him of both a past and a future he had experienced but until then had forgotten. Soon after he had stood under the highway bridge and seen the vision that would send him out into the land, the woman in the photograph enrolled in his class as a student. She'd been a stewardess who'd married a third officer, been divorced, and become a photographer. Her name was Nancy. Eventually she and her teacher became lovers.

In spite of her, McWilliams left on his travels every month, like an orphan, bereft, like a man with no home. He crossed and recrossed the South, from Tennessee to Savannah to Florida to New Orleans to Texas and then back to Louisiana. From Macon to Montezuma to Panama City to Key West. Down the Ohio, from Pittsburgh through Louisville and Cairo to Memphis. Into Alabama, up to Chattanooga, then down to the Delta. West Texas, north Georgia, south Georgia, and West Virginia. Eastern Kentucky and South Carolina. Mobile, Cartersville, Nashville, and the Gulf. Everywhere, looking for signs, circling the cities, hanging out on the periphery, looking in, from the edge in the afternoon, in the long shadows, in the golden light, watching the towns grow out of the ground, the ground just broken and

unresolved, a chaos, a dump scattered with old machines and refuse. Whenever he could, he'd find a graveyard, as still and stable as a magnetic pole, a vantage point, due north, where he could set up his tripod and watch the earth wheel around, encompassing a zone of meaning. Once, in a graveyard near Dallas, he saw an angel walking in a family plot, trapped under a cage. Once, near Macon, he saw two boys made of limestone, one holding a book, the other sitting on a tasseled throne, looking across at a warehouse. Along the Texas-Louisiana border he came upon a pasture of dead cows, and beyond that, a seashore scattered with dead dolphins, the whole region a purgatory, an ultimate destination, where everything washed out east of the Mississippi came to rest, unresolved.

McWilliams started making photographs of generating plants, factories, and mines, images of power and inhuman scale, pictures of cooling towers bigger than the castles of walled cities, filling the sky with man-made clouds, of smokestacks, taller and more tapered than obelisks, of mills that stretched from one side of the horizon to the other, their huge buildings white like chalk cliffs in the sun. Again and again he made pictures of immense piles of sand and gravel, man-made mountains, half-hidden in fogs of dust and smoke, fed by huge derricks, their peaks shadowed by storm clouds. Like a man wandering through a landscape of towers, pyramids, and ziggurats, he began to notice signs of an impending judgment. He began to photograph empty billboards, glowing in the afternoon light, bare of messages, as if they were the walls of a palace, waiting for the finger of God to trace a warning and he were Daniel, waiting to read it. In Florida he came upon two men standing on a ladder, wrapping a shroud around something that might once have been a building. In Kentucky at sunset, under low clouds, he saw another man leaning against the skeletal frame of an old house that, in the gloom, looked as if it were being built while it was being destroyed. In Texas he photographed a grove of gnarled and twisted trees, torn up by a tornado. The storm had scattered branches everywhere, creating a strange, prickly landscape that had been made in an instant but, in the photograph, appeared to have been there forever, whole and unchanged. In Tennessee he came upon a strip mine, as broad and deep as the Grand Canyon, that looked in the photograph as if it were a hole dug by a four-year-old playing in his own backyard. Again and again he saw small stagnant lakes in Florida, Tennessee, and Arkansas, pools of brackish water, rimmed with dead fish and pine trees, that he photographed as if they were mirrors, bisecting the land and sky, doubling the clouds and the groves along their banks, looking as pure and peaceful as the translucent coves, bays, and freshwater inlets of nineteenth-century New England, painted by such luminists as FitzHugh Lane.

Over and over he used his camera to change the wrecks of abandoned buildings and old factories into the ruins of a civilization through which he passed like a poet reciting "Ozymandias." The poured concrete façade of an unfinished motel in South Carolina became part of a Mayan temple complex overgrown with vines. An old stone water tower north of Atlanta became the only battlement that remained of a demolished castle in Scotland. Ruined brick mausoleums by a river in Macon; a burned-out courthouse in Arkansas, farmland, half-flooded by a new dam that looked like dry land just emerging from the Deluge; an empty ball park in a landscape poisoned by acid fumes from a smelter; a pair of tennis shoes, tied together, hanging on a power line above a deserted coastal road, like debris left by the receding waters of a great flood—all became part of a present seen as if it were part of a past that grew more and more remote with every photograph he made.

He began to find things that looked like fossils. Outside Memphis the ground opened up, and he saw huge concrete pipes, lying unearthed in an excavation like the bones of a great beast. In the coalfields of eastern Kentucky he discovered the broken scoop of a strip-mining shovel, its bucket and hinged lower jaw crushed like the skull of a monstrous pig. In the winter in West Virginia he came upon the hood of an old truck, turned upside down on the ground, like the carapace of a great turtle.

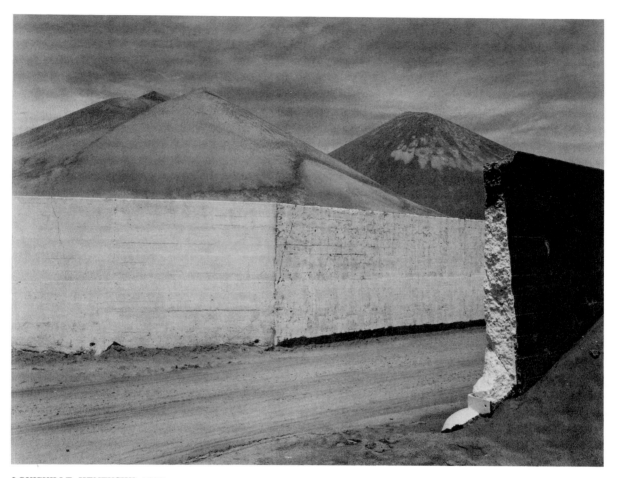

LOUISVILLE, KENTUCKY, 1975

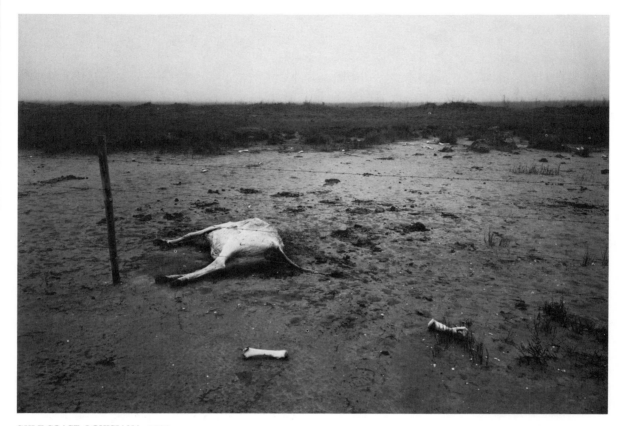

GULF COAST, LOUISIANA, 1976

In Charleston, on the beach, he saw piles of shattered concrete infested with worms of rusted steel. In one junkyard in Nashville he discovered a petrified tree, growing straight up out of the ground, made of the tall section of an airplane, and in another junkyard he came upon a huge letter A that seemed to have been frozen in flight by some catastrophe.

Time receded as he watched. Power plants turned to ruins; machines turned to fossils; the land heaved and smoked and steamed. He saw the mountains of eastern Kentucky, shrouded in mist, dense with vines turning into a green, primordial landscape inhabited by tree sloths, monkeys, and parrots. He walked into caves of limestone quarries that looked like places where men, hunted by tigers, took refuge. On a vast mud flat, cleared of trees for an industrial park, he photographed eroded crisscrossed tracks that looked as if they had been made not by earthmovers but by dinosaurs. In the high light of noon he saw eroded shapes floating on the surface of water-filled strip mines like giant segmented worms. At twilight he watched as these pools of water, surrounded by dark, barren land, glowed like the warm, moonlit seas of an earth whose only life forms were plankton. In eighteen months he had gone so deep beneath the surface, so far into the shadows, that, like Frederick Church, the great nineteenth-century American landscape painter who had traveled to Ecuador and the Andes to apprehend and to paint the face of God revealed in stone, McWilliams had seen and recorded a vision of primordial nature, untouched by humans. Just as Church's great teacher, Thomas Cole, had painted a series of monumental canvases whose subject was titled the "Course of Empire," so McWilliams had recorded the trajectory of a whole civilization. But unlike Cole, whose first canvas had depicted a classical scene of bucolic innocence and whose last was of a vast Carthaginian ruin, and unlike Church, who had had to travel to the tropics to discover a landscape that still bore evidence of its divine origin, McWilliams had remained in America and there discovered and documented a contemporary paradox whose contradictions were astounding: In the very process of creating the future, men were creating not only ruins but fossils, and not just fossils but a primordial past. McWilliams, the prophet, had seen the future, and the future resembled the very beginning of time.

McWilliams returned to Atlanta, glowing like a fire. Ariel had stuffed all his possessions in garbage bags and left them on the curb. The wind blew his birth certificate down the street, but it hardly mattered. He had created an immense transcendent body of work; not only was his job waiting for him, but he was given tenure; Nancy was in love with him; Carter was still President; and Nexus, the brainchild of Stewart, had applied for and been granted unprecedented sums of money by agencies as di-

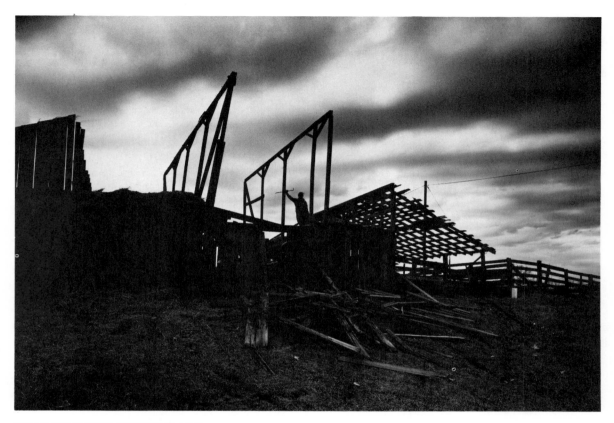

DISMANTLED BARN, KENTUCKY, 1976

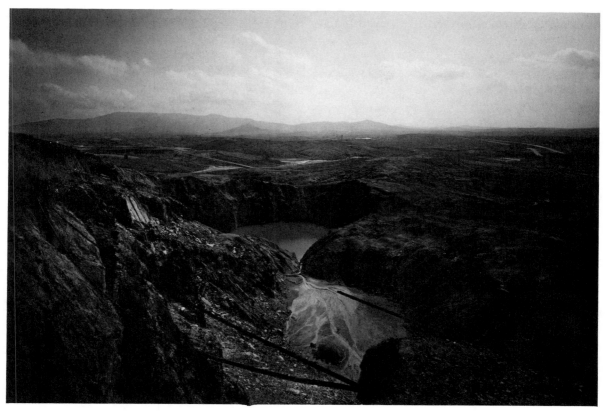

COPPERHILL, TENNESSEE, 1977

verse as the Department of Labor and the National Endowment for the Arts. Protected by his former employer, the Black Prince, who was himself the protégé and heir apparent of the city's mayor, Stewart had only to reach for the phone to talk to those he described as "our friends in important places." The finest cocaine had replaced the best marijuana as the drug-of-choice conversation. The whole city of Atlanta, a city whose symbol was the phoenix, seemed to glint and glimmer in the sun like a jeweled bird. McWilliams decided he had a mission: to chronicle the way modern humankind touched and was touched by the earth. In the fall of 1978 he declared that his next journey would be to Alaska. Unfortunately he didn't realize that he and his friends were as much the creatures of the civilization he had recorded as the builders of power plants, the owners of strip mines, and the holders of public office.

McWilliams devised a plan that might have pleased his New England ancestor King Caesar, the Haverhill who had built ships and engaged in the Triangular Trade. He called it the Alaska Venture. In return for $500 he promised each of ten investors a portfolio of photographs made in Alaska. By the spring of 1979 he had sold his shares and fitted out his truck. At the same time, in partnership with Nexus, he had convinced the executive committee of the Atlanta Arts Festival to employ him and Stewart and the Nexus staff to rebuild

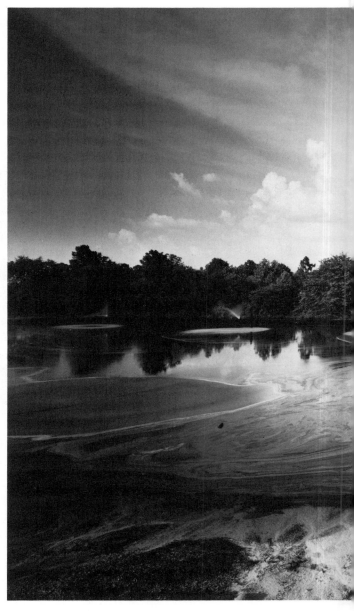

CREOSOTE POND, ALABAMA, 1977

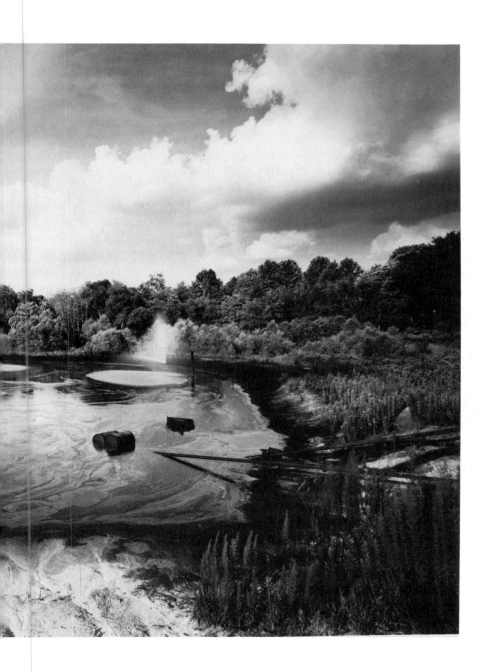

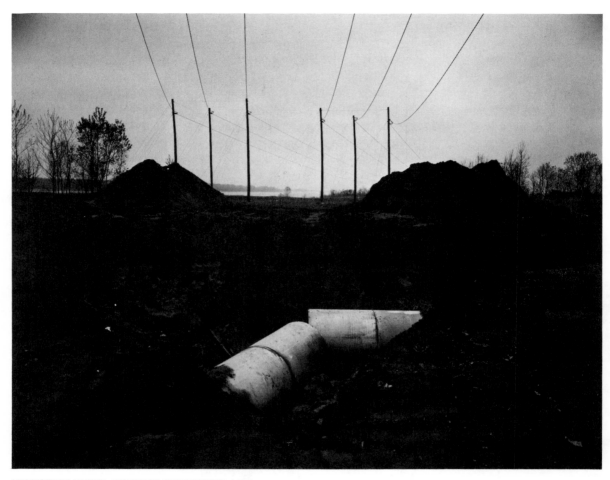

MISSISSIPPI RIVER, MEMPHIS, TENNESSEE, 1970

and refurbish the festival's central pavilion. With $5,000 in his pocket and his credentials freshly stamped by the patrons, collectors, and civic leaders of the Festival Committee as a member in good standing, he kissed his girl friend and his children good-bye and headed north, thinking, *How clever! How resourceful! What a Compleat Angler I am!* Thirty miles from the city he started screaming, "What have I done?" He didn't want to leave; he didn't want to be alone; he didn't want to drive 6,000 miles into a wilderness. The little boy who was scared of heights, the ten-year-old who had been sent away to the top of a mountain, the little kid who was scared of the dark began to cry. McWilliams pulled off the road and wept. All he wanted to do was go home, but he couldn't. He'd sold the shares and made the deals. He wiped his face and started again. He was supposed to be a man with a mission, the new Leif Ericsson! So what was he? (He was holding the wheel so tight that his knuckles were white.) A chickenshit? He was going north to Alaska! He was going to climb the tallest mountain, stand there, and recite, "I am the master of my fate: I am the captain of my soul." Loneliness was part of the deal; it came with the territory. He kept driving. His knuckles stayed white until he reached Anchorage.

He had a list of names and started calling. No one was home, or no one was interested. Finally, he called a guy named Frankie Lee. Frankie had once lived in At-

lanta. A good old boy, with a wife and two kids. He had had himself a bank job, a nice house, a promising career. Came from a good family, too. He'd just chucked it and got a job on the pipeline. Frankie Lee said, "Sure! Come on by!" The first thing he did was show McWilliams his two ID's: in one hand, a Georgia driver's license, complete with picture of Mr. Suburbia; in the other, his Alaska pipeline ID, illustrated with the face of a hairy, bug-eyed madman. Frankie Lee invited McWilliams for a drink. He introduced him to all his friends. They were just like Frankie Lee: $50,000-a-year working stiffs, formerly married, previously white-collar, separated from their kids, full of regrets, loaded with alcohol. McWilliams wondered what he was doing there. If he was really Leif Ericsson, then where were all the Davy Crocketts?

He started roaming and discovered that the frontier was long gone. The land was there, wild and massive, but the feds or the oil companies or the Eskimos owned it. The place was scattered with guys from the lower forty-eight who'd come apart at the seams. He'd seen it before: Southern Florida was littered with people's last hot dog stands. Alaska was dotted with shacks and whiskey dreams. And there *he* was, driving around in his cute little truck, brewing himself a nice pot of tea every morning like some Englishman on safari. Guys would ask him if he was looking for work, and he'd say no, no, he was just taking pictures, and they'd reach for their beer, say-

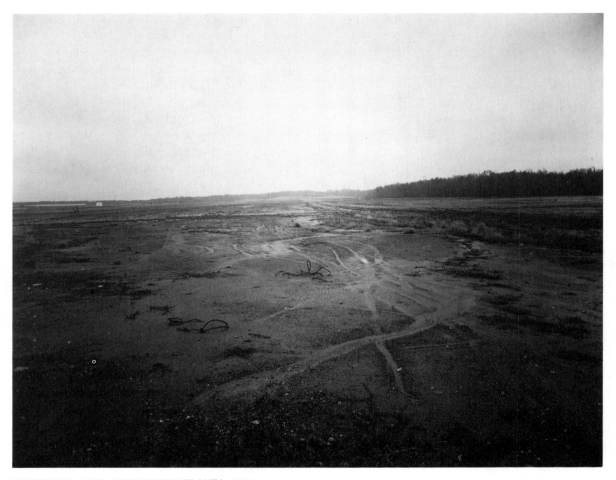

INDUSTRIAL PARK, SOUTHWEST ATLANTA, 1976

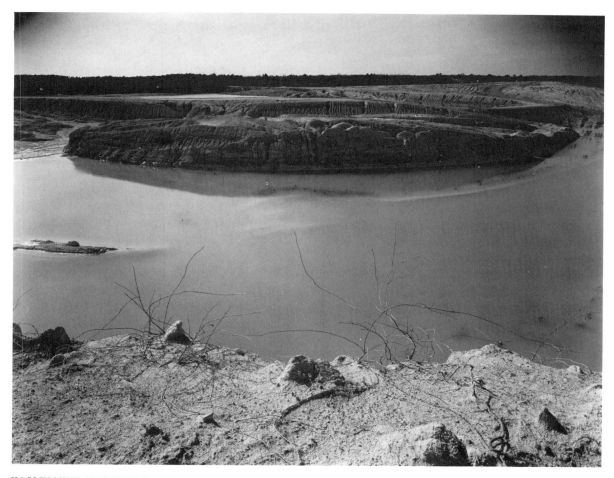

KAOLIN MINE, WASHINGTON COUNTY, GEORGIA, 1975

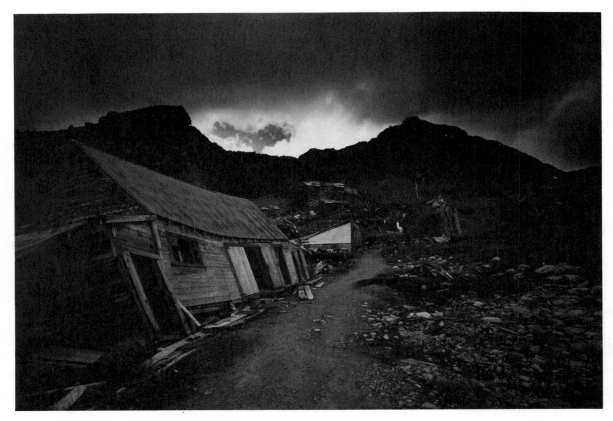

THATCHER PASS GOLD MINE, ALASKA, 1979

ing, "What the hell for?" He started lying. He was there, he said, working on a grant from the National Endowment for the Arts. It made him feel worse than ever. It proved he didn't know who he was and what he was doing there.

He tried taking pictures of the pipeline, that miracle of American engineering, that marvel of resourcefulness. He couldn't do it. "I looked at it from every fuckin' point of view," he said, "and could not take a picture of it. Not one. It looked like a thread stretched across Manhattan. It was that absurd in relation to the land. It was nothing. Men couldn't make the significant kind of marks in Alaska they could in the South. They were so far away from their center of supply, and the land was so awesome that their marks were pathetic. No matter what they did, the mountains were always there, overwhelming and uncompromising. I couldn't make my old arguments again. My camera was no good to me. It was an inadequate device. Even my five-by-seven. I couldn't do it. The place was too big, too grand, too picture-postcard perfect." Still, he tried. Two thousand times. He drove where he could, flew where he couldn't. But too often the paradoxical balance that he'd discovered and carried with him from the South—the subtle, contradictory equation between gestures of creation and gestures of destruction, between a technological future and a simultaneous primordial past— tipped in favor of primordial nature, in favor of a bleak, bitter hopelessness. Pa-

thetic little pumps stood abandoned on the edges of glacial valleys, old gold-mining shacks stretched like ringworm along the bases of mountains, and abandoned trucks lay like driftwood along the shores. He missed his children. And he missed Nancy. He was no loner and no outlaw.

When, at last, he found his mountain and reached the top, all he felt was "faded. I had a sense of being on a tired globe. With airplanes circling and subways running from one town to the next. With people who yawn as they fly from one side of the earth to the other. There was no mystery to it anymore. I stood on the top of a hill, connected by roads, and I got in my car and drove off. I felt there was a threshold I still couldn't cross, a threshold of fear, of throwing myself *into* the elements and of surviving without the need to control. Of living for the moment. Of being there. I couldn't do it. Couldn't do it. And photography couldn't do it for me. Up until that time I believed it could. Photography was just a shitty little crutch, a poor little tool, that couldn't manage the real task: to be able to be *alive.* To stuff some food in my pockets and walk twenty miles across the tundra, into the hills, and live for a week—I couldn't do that. I felt all the rivers were dammed, everything was controlled. I could get in my car and drive to Alaska. I could get on a plane and fly to the other side of the world. I could pick up my camera and give form. But all the mysteries and mistakes were gone. I controlled the thing too much. I didn't make any mistakes anymore. Photography had been a revelation. Photography had made me whole. But I'd mastered it, and it couldn't give me anything more. I had to come out from behind it."

He drove home, thinking about certain kinds of freedom and certain kinds of limits. When he reached Atlanta, he asked Nancy if she'd marry him. A year later three things happened almost at once: Jimmy Carter lost the election; all the fat checks sent from Washington to Nexus suddenly stopped; and the Black Prince, who had been Stewart's protector, lost a local election and left Stewart without protection. In the process of turning Nexus from a storefront gallery into an organization with a six-figure annual budget, Stewart had made a few enemies. After the checks had stopped and his protection disappeared, Stewart discovered that the survival of an arts organization directed by whites was not considered crucial by the local black politicians who now ran a city with barely enough money to pay its police and feed its poor. Hard times and old enemies turned Stewart gray, bitter, and a little crazy. He pleaded with McWilliams to represent the organization at public meetings that resembled hunting scenes. City councilmen called Stewart a fascist. Neighborhood groups shouted he was a racist. For a year McWilliams met with lawyers and trustees and sat through meeting after meeting, fending off lawsuits, rumors, and committee inquiries. When it was over, Stewart had been nearly buried in the rubble, and McWilliams had begun to think that the safest place to be was as far out in the open as possible. It had been two years since he'd returned to Atlanta, and he hadn't taken any new pictures.

Six months after Nancy had given birth to their first child, McWilliams cleared all the brush from his backyard and began to build a boat, a double-ended, single-masted, twenty-four-foot vessel capable of ocean voyages, its hull of laminated cedar and mahogany. A landscape photographer who had seen too much, he turned from the land; the offspring of sea traders, early settlers, and western travelers, he was like Ishmael, at the beginning of *Moby Dick*, headed for the open sea. "How I spurned that turnpike earth," Ishmael had said, "that common highway, all over dented with the marks of slavish heels and hoofs; and turned me to admire the magnanimity of the sea which will permit no records." The descendant of a man blown ashore in a shipwreck and of another who had bought and sold whole valleys, McWilliams was an American looking for a new beginning *and* a safe haven, for sanctuary *and* risk, building one home while searching for a new one, wandering along an edge, thinking about China and dreaming about the moon.

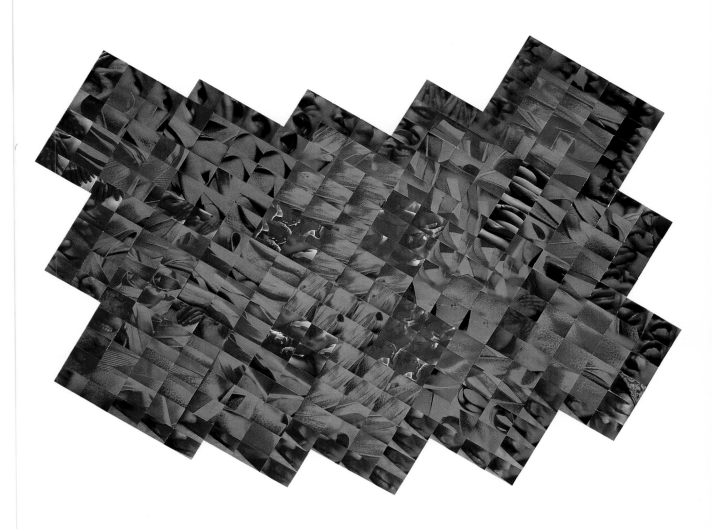

SURROGATE LOVE, 1977

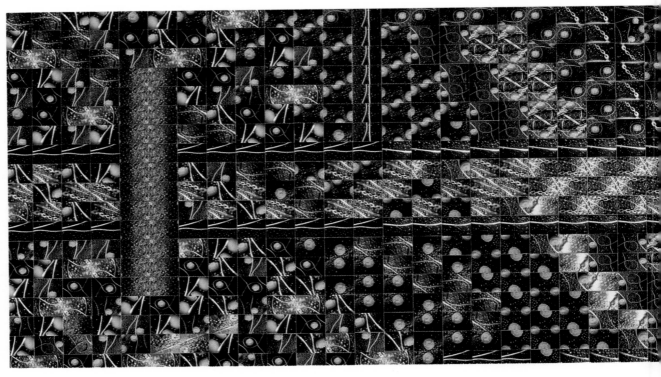

TATSUNOKUCHI: FACE OF THE UNIVERSE, 1980, IN THE COLLECTION OF
J. PATRICK LANNAN FOUNDATION MUSEUM, PALM BEACH, FLORIDA

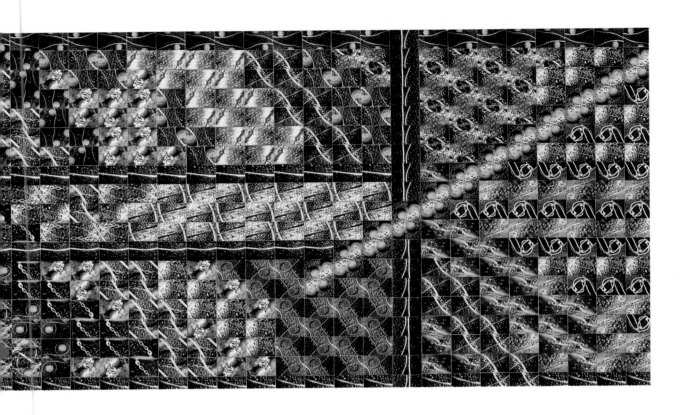

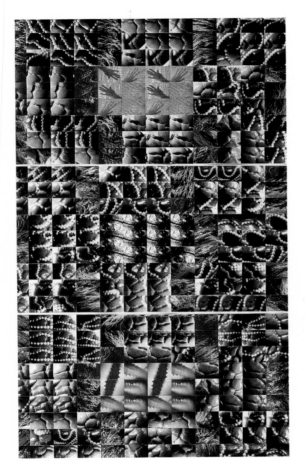

TRIBAL GIFTS, 1978

DIAMOND PRECEPT, 1979

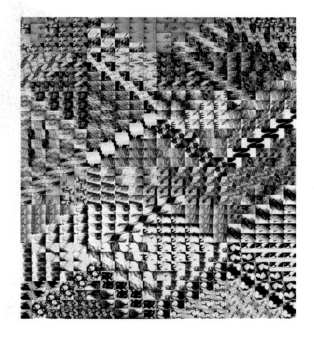

en years ago a university hired me to teach history, but the only people I met were photographers who were earning graduate degrees in art. They were all one thing, and I was another. The department I was in was so genteel that it had a sherry budget; its classrooms were in buildings with Gothic courtyards; outside one was a statue of Nathan Hale, a handsome young man, standing with his arms bound, waiting to be shot by the British, his last words of regret inscribed at his feet. The building where the artists and photographers had their studios and darkrooms was different: It was so brutally modern, with ceilings so low, rooms so dark and concrete so un-finished that soon after it had opened, it was set on fire, out of revenge, either by a painter, a photographer, or an architecture student; no one knew who, but many were willing to take the credit.

The day I arrived to meet my department chairman for the first time, he was late, so I waited for him in his office, surrounded by old oak Windsor chairs, textbooks, and dust. An old man with a white beard, dressed in tweeds, with a new Polaroid in a leather case slung from his shoulder, padded in and sat down across from me. The secretary came in to ask if he'd like a cup of tea. He said he would, and then, very carefully, he lifted something wrapped in a white linen handkerchief out of his pocket. He laid it on the table, and with just the tips of his fingers, he began delicately to unwrap it as if it were something fragile that had been damaged. He looked to me so much like Clifford, the beautiful old man in Hawthorne's *The House of the Seven Gables*, that I thought what he had in the handkerchief was perhaps an old painted miniature or even a daguerreotype. Soon he finished, and with a wonderfully happy smile, he held it up to show it to me: It was a can of Coke that had been run over by a truck. Just then the secretary returned and introduced me to Walker Evans. Since my chairman still hadn't arrived, we talked. Evans said he had taught photography at the university for some time but had just retired. The people in photography, he said, were ever so much more interesting than the people in history. He told me to visit. When I did, the people I met knew my work. Since they knew I studied photographs as if they were documents, they trusted me enough to let me look and listen while they talked about the pictures they made. That's how I eventually met Andrea.

She was the youngest of the graduate students working on master's degrees in photography. The oldest, maybe the wisest, certainly the quietest, was an ex-marine named Peter who'd spent too much time at Khe Sanh, watching North Vietnamese shells come in while the helicopters lifted out the stretcher cases and the body bags. After Peter had got back, he stayed either in his darkroom or in the woods, making pictures of boulders sunk under an ocean of silence. There was one woman named Marsha Dew, whose name fitted her manner so well that to pronounce it was to call up the picture of someone so clear-eyed and open-faced that instead of perfume, she seemed to wear the fragrance of freshly washed and ironed cotton. There was another woman named Christine, a lapsed Polish Catholic from Chicago, whose sisters were nuns; she made pictures of herself, pale and thin, floating in a big, white enamel bathtub, as innocently naked as a child in a baptismal font. There was a young photographer from San Francisco, the child of a man who'd fled his village in China at the end of the Second World War and then named his newborn children after the Hollywood movie stars he admired the most. His son, Reagan, made gray monochromatic minimalist pictures of things like cinder blocks resting on the grass; when people asked him to explain what he did, Reagan kept so stubbornly silent that if the question was repeated, it took on the sound of an insult to his intelligence. Another young man named Wallace wanted to be famous so badly that it seemed as if he made his pictures with a copy of *Artforum* in one hand and a French jounal of semiotics in the other; Wallace hung out at small airports, making enigmatic pictures of such signs and signifiers as runway lights, wind socks, and taxi and takeoff instructions. There was even a conventionally well-bred young man from Georgia named Charles, a secret reader of Ouspensky, who loved to go to strange, dark, and deserted places like construction sites and parking lots in the middle of the night, where he'd open fire with a big strobe for one-sixtieth of a second, never knowing what he'd photographed until after he'd returned home, developed his film, and printed it.

And then there was Andrea. Kindhearted, understanding women of a certain age from the South would have shaken their heads and called her a handful. Healthy young men of any region would also have shaken their heads and then headed either straight for her or straight away, depending on their ages and previous experiences. Andrea was twenty years old, dark-haired, dark-eyed, pale-skinned, as round and pretty as a Russian doll, but with a wit as cruel, quick, precise, informed, and ribald as an eighteenth-century lady, fluttering behind her fan at a court ball. Andrea would take a seat at a table in her favorite gay bar, and with a crowd of men around her and enough alcohol in her, she could talk about herself, her friends, and her enemies, about books and poetry and painting, as if she were speed-reading from a TelePrompTer whose lines were whizzing past her like stock market quotations during the busiest day of a wild bull market. No fly could settle on a glass, no car could pass on the street, no hand could reach for a match without its turning into her next line. Often those who had begun laughing, thinking that she was talking about someone else, discovered, between breaths, that she was talking about them. Just as often, though, she talked about herself, with the crazed wit of someone making nervous jokes while standing on the trapdoor of a gallows—jokes that everyone laughed at out of revenge or embarrassment or relief or even out of amazement that someone who claimed to be so unhappy could be so demonstrably witty.

Andrea lived all alone in an apartment whose bathroom she had slathered with metallic silver paint, so that, what with the pink of her tub, toilet, and sink and the black tiles that bordered them, to walk into that little room was like stepping into a 1957 Ford Thunderbird equipped with a white toy poodle wearing a rhinestone collar. Her kitchen was always bare; her refrigerator, always empty of everything except a quart of orange soda and a large hand-painted plastic goldfish lying on its side. All that, combined with the disarray of her bedroom and the Polaroid pictures of various faces and bodies scattered about, made some of her more innocent visitors think they'd blundered onto the set of *Pink Flamingos,* an underground film whose star was a 300-pound transvestite named Divine. Andrea's own sexuality always seemed somewhat in doubt, although her affections clearly included herself. When she wasn't alone or holding court at the bar, she spent time with a gay poet named

René Ricard, an émigré from Warhol's Factory who had been the subject of a hit pop song in the sixties, a song called "Walk Away, Renée," which is what he often did best, as Andrea first noticed one night when she called out that he had the most beautiful ass in the world. When she wasn't with René and his boyfriend, Andrea was with her girl friend Marjorie, a blonde painter who sometimes appeared in Andrea's pictures as Andrea, just as Andrea sometimes appeared, with the right wig, as Marjorie.

For two years no one quite knew what sort of pictures Andrea was making. Everyone knew she made them with a $10 Polaroid she'd bought in a drugstore. Everyone also knew that they were autobiographical and that her motto was "The bigger the better." A few people had heard that she liked medical photography, but even they were unsettled by the invitation she sent out to announce her thesis show. Beneath the title, "Andrea Kovács Shows Alone," she had reproduced a medical photograph of a hand without an index finger, the very finger photographers use to press their shutters. If the finger had been surgically removed and the wound repaired or if it had simply been missing because of a birth defect, the picture might have been disquieting but bearable—some sophisticated people might have even called it interesting—but the picture Andrea chose as her emblem was that of a hand whose finger had rotted off and been replaced by a fistula that looked exactly like an eye staring out from where the knuckle had been. A shutter finger had become an open wound that was an eye. Most people agreed, of course, that anguish had long been a subject of high art, but even the Grünewald "Crucifixion" had been only one painting, while Andrea was said to have enough work to fill the Art Building's main gallery. This would have been difficult enough for anyone, since as low, dark, narrow, and constricted as every other room in the Art Building was, its gallery was so grandly proportioned that the only thing that could fill it without being dwarfed was either a small circus or a major abstract expressionist retrospective. How Andrea would fill it with a bunch of Polaroids made with a plastic camera was hard to imagine. The prospect that she'd fill it with pictures metaphorically equivalent to the one she'd used for her invitation was a bit frightening. She did manage it, though.

On every wall were huge panels of images, some large, some small, fitted side by side like mosaics in a grid. Some were made of eight or ten black-and-whites, each enlarged to four feet by six feet. Others were composed of hundreds of little color Polaroids, taped together in rows, one on top of the other, to form rectangles six feet high and fifteen feet long. To the left of the gallery entrance, Andrea had placed eight black-and-white enlargements of what, from a distance, looked like aerial photographs of the terrain of a barren high plateau, crisscrossed here and there by some sort of furrowed tracks. Up close they turned into patches of Andrea's skin that she'd scratched with a nail file and then photographed under high magnification. To the left of this was a long wall of black-and-white blowups of Andrea and a young man—pictures that seemed to have been made at very close range by two lovers of each other as they floated on a wave of sex. Next to these was the first of the Polaroid mosaics. Some of these were the originals from which Andrea had made the blowups of herself and her lover; others were pictures of Andrea's hand, pushing, pulling, and kneading her own flesh as if it were taffy or rising dough. On the facing wall was another set of Polaroids that looked at first like duplicates of the others but, close up, were pictures of Andrea's hand touching, pressing, then grabbing at the flesh of a man and a woman. Between these facing grids of Polaroids was the back wall of the gallery, which people saw when they walked in. For many, it was both the first and the last thing they saw, since as soon as they came in, they turned around and left. They did that because it was covered with a double row of mural-size black-and-white prints of Andrea's hand, the fingers tipped with long, pointed black nails, not just grabbing and holding the soft flesh of what might have been her thigh, but pulling apart and then clawing open the lips of her vagina. The pictures were so explicit but so cold and clinical that those who

weren't embarrassed were repelled. The rest of the gallery was filled with variations on the themes of desire and narcissism. There was another wall of blowups of Andrea touching the body of a young man who seemed to be asleep and a final, monumental wall of Polaroids, a collection of faces, places, bodies, and gestures of everyone and everything that had either directly or indirectly influenced or been incorporated by the show: Marjorie was there wearing sunglasses; René and his boyfriend were there with their backs turned and their heads cut off; Andrea's hand showed up again, all by itself; so did people like Charles, Wallace, and Reagan. There were even snapshots of the two men Andrea had touched. One of them was an art school dropout who was trying to start his own rock and roll band. Andrea invited him to the opening only because he had some records she wanted to play.

Some who saw the work dismissed it as an exercise in anguished narcissism. Others said Andrea was an exhibitionist. Andrea, of course, had her own theories and legitimizations: one was to point to the body art of Vito Acconci, an artist who had done such things as build a false floor in an otherwise empty gallery and then lie under it, silently waiting like a troll until people unwittingly walked in and over him, looking for the art they'd come to see. Once they were in the gallery, he'd announce through a loudspeaker that not only was he, the artist, trapped beneath them, but out of loneliness and desire, he was masturbating while he thought of them. If that allusion wasn't convincing enough, Andrea had another: Her Polaroid grids were in sympathy with the work of the French novelist Alain Robbe-Grillet, a writer, she said, who used words instead of a camera to scan his surroundings and used these scans to create near-photographic sequences of reality, full of repetition and variation whose totality, she said, "was a hard, phenomenological cocoon at whose center was the mind of a single human being." Her mind, she said, quoting Robert Rauschenberg, was a "flatbed of impressions" on which everything left its mark. She was using her camera to bring her insides out, so she could look at them.

That's what she claimed, but I couldn't believe it. Her pictures had no more life in them than Reagan's cinder blocks or Wallace's semiotic little airports. Andrea pushed and pulled at her flesh as if it were dead; she looked so closely at her own skin that it changed from a membrane of touch into a landscape seen from a distance; she examined her genitals with as much care as a veterinary gynecologist. The man she seemed to float with on a wave of sex was actually a Vietnam veteran so damaged by what had happened to him and so deadened by alternate doses of lithium and Thorazine that he couldn't even lift his feet off the ground when he walked. The other man she grabbed at was asleep, and the woman she touched was nothing but her double.

The pictures she made of René and his boyfriend she called "Love and Death by Attrition"; the pictures she made of her own hand gesturing alone she called "Talking to the Blind." She made images of intimacy as big as billboards that couldn't be seen except from a distance; she made images of flesh so monstrous that they took on the dead weight of a nightmare. She claimed her pictures came from the inside out, but every one of them looked as if it had been made by someone on the outside, trying to get in. Ten days after her show opened, Henry Geldzahler, then curator of contemporary painting at the Metropolitan Museum of Art, came to the university for a visit. He looked at Andrea's show and came back again, this time in the company of Ellsworth Kelly, a postwar American abstractionist who made elegant minimal but monumental paintings inspired by such natural elements as the curve of a leaf reduced to its essential form. Kelly looked at the enlargements Andrea had made of her skin and her genitals, and for a moment, art and life went their separate ways: He said her pictures were wonderful. With that aesthetic blessing she left the university, moved to New York, and then, for ten years, she disappeared.

She didn't vanish, though. People would see her on the street or at openings; someone said she'd even had a show at an uptown gallery. Every few years I'd talk to her on the phone; one time she told me she was in love with a Greek hot dog vendor.

Once I heard she'd had a big piece in a show at the New Museum in SoHo. I called her to ask about it; she said she'd sold it to a collector from West Palm Beach. Then she asked me if I chanted. I said, "What?" and she said something like "Nam yoho ringeh k'yo." I thought of "anna nisi masa," the nonsense phrase that keeps running through the mind of the film director in Fellini's *8½*. She said, "Say it"; I said, "No"; she said, "Go ahead." So I did, and then she laughed and said, "Congratulations, you're a bodhisattva." I asked what that was, and she said it was a saint. I'd always thought it was harder to do than that. I asked her what the words meant, and she said they were "All devotion to the Lotus Sutra." *Ah! The Lotus Sutra!* I thought. *Andrea's made her journey to the East.* I couldn't imagine it though: Andrea standing in an airport with a peaceful smile and a copy of *Lord Krishna, the Blue God,* handing out red paper poppies to innocent guys who'd just got off the plane on leave after eight weeks of basic training. Andrea was too smart for that. And as Kelly and Geldzahler had noticed, she was too much of an artist. I'd heard the piece in the New Museum was a twenty-three-foot-long photomosaic made of 1,000 separate images. She couldn't do that and be blissed-out at the same time. What had happened to René and Marjorie and the poodle with the rhinestones and the lady fluttering behind her fan? What had become of all the dead flesh and the desperate gestures? I asked her if she'd show me her work. It had been ten years, and I was curious. She invited me over.

She lived on Eighth Street, west of Fifth Avenue, in the same block as Jimi Hendrix's Electric Lady recording studio, three flights up, over a shop that sold T-shirts with "I love N.Y." written in Japanese. When I got there, she said, "Oh! Good! You're just in time; I'm about to do my morning gongyo." I didn't know what to do. Take off my shoes? Cover my head? Cover my eyes? Walk around the block? She invited me in. I could sit; she'd chant, and then we'd talk. There was a little kitchen and a bathroom and one room with gigantic windows that filled the place with perfect north light.

I sat down at one end of the room, and she knelt at the other with her back to me, facing a beautiful black lacquer cabinet. Across its top was a latticework of intricately carved lotus blossoms. In the center, between them, was a gilded medallion of a crane with its wings raised in a circle above its head; Andrea told me it was a sign of good luck and protection. The cabinet stood on a table covered with a piece of black glass that glistened like a lake in the dark. Andrea lit a stick of incense and put it in a little wooden box in front of the cabinet. On either side were candles, and on either side of them were vases with freshly cut greens. On the right was a bowl of fruit. As the incense smoked, she struck a brass bell, cupped upside down in the petals of a gilded lotus on a stand. She hit the bell twice, rapidly, and as the vibration filled the room, she opened the doors of the cabinet. Inside were two more doors, inlaid and gilded, held shut by a clasp shaped like a flying crane. In front of these doors was a miniature table on which stood two black cups, shaped like eggs. In one was pure water; in the other, clean rice. Andrea opened the inner doors. For some reason I expected to see the Oriental equivalent of a madonna or a saint. Instead, there was a scroll of calligraphy hanging from a hook, held flat by two more of the crane medallions. Down the center of the scroll was a text whose characters moved like a wiring diagram that had come alive. Andrea struck the bell again, and like a singer with a pitchpipe, she began to chant in harmony with the bell's overtones.

At first, for a few beats, the chant sounded as grand as an aria in a requiem mass, but then its tempo changed like a tape switched to fast forward, except that each word remained clear. The words were the same ones she had said to me on the phone, but she was chanting them over and over again, in a cycle that beat up and out of her not like a refrain, but like a rapid wave form traced by light on an oscilloscope, like a pattern of energy displayed on a monitor that translated heartbeat, blood pressure, and respiration into peaks and valleys of blue light that continued and continued and continued. I had spent enough time in darkrooms, counting to myself as I developed film to keep track of how long she went from one breath to the next and how many accented beats there were in each cycle. Four times a second, every ten seconds, Andrea's breath pulsed out of her like a hand beating a drum.

Andrea was chanting a mantra, one I hadn't heard before. All mantras, I knew, were religious, and all were composed of words and phrases called seed syllables that were believed to activate different energy centers of the body, centers the Hindus called *charkas*, or lotus centers. Mantras had been used for thousands of years for purposes of self-enlightenment in India and Tibet by Hindus, then in China and Japan by Buddhists. The compound sounds of the Hindu mantra "om" were intended to activate and unify the waking, dreaming, and deep-sleeping centers of consciousness, but Andrea's chanting was so rapid and percussive that whatever the mantra was, it was clearly not intended to put her to sleep. I thought of the "hare krishna, hare rama" chant, in which "ram" was used to activate the energy center near the heart, but I still couldn't understand why Andrea was doing what she was doing. And then I remembered the story J. D. Salinger had told about Franny Glass: Franny was a perfectly nice young woman, a child prodigy of a family of prodigies, who one day, for no good reason, suddenly got sick of food and sick of her boyfriend at college and even sick of college. She came home, took to bed, and started silently to recite "Lord Jesus Christ have mercy on me" over and over again. She'd learned it from a little book called *The Way of the Pilgrim,* which told the story of a Russian peasant who'd traveled everywhere, trying to discover a way to pray without ceasing, until one day he met an old monk who told him that if he repeated the words "Lord Jesus Christ . . ." over and over, they'd eventually synchronize with his heart. That sounded just fine to me; if Franny could do it, so could Andrea. Everyone was entitled to a religious awakening. But Andrea was an artist, and artists are people with no padding at all between themselves and the road and very little distance between who they think and feel they are and what they actually do with that understanding. When I'd known Andrea at the university, she'd been in a lot of trouble, and the work had shown it, maybe even more than she knew. If the chanting had activated something inside her, the next question was about the work that had to have come out.

She chanted for twenty minutes; by the end she'd switched to another text, a long one that never repeated itself but that rushed forward in rapid alliterated bursts of such speed and clarity that her voice took on the beat of an electric typewriter wired to a computer. At the end she struck the bell in the lotus twice and intoned the original mantra with the same operatic grandeur as she had in the beginning. Then, in the voice of a little girl who'd just been given a glass of milk and a cookie, she said "Thank you" to the scroll and closed the doors of the cabinet. She turned and smiled; outside, the traffic roared its way east, across town.

We sat and looked at each other for a while, and then I asked her if she had anything to show me. She said she had a lot, but she wanted to begin with something she'd done soon after she'd started chanting in the presence of the scroll she called her Gohonzon. She opened a storage cabinet and pulled out a photomosaic, folded over and over on itself like a blanket. She asked me to help her spread it out on the floor. It was as wide as her room. It was so big that I had to stand on a stool to see it, and when I did, it was so astonishing that for a moment I forgot where I was and stepped back and nearly fell. It was a pattern as intricate as a Persian rug and as variegated as a snakeskin. There must have been 500 separate color photographs in it. Wave forms zigzagged across it from left to right; crystalline shapes, faceted like diamonds, appeared and disappeared into and out of it. I thought of tracks left by lightning bolts in silica sand; I thought of a crystal lattice marked by an electrical charge that had been trapped within it; I thought of light that reverberated, was bent, broken, and held within a gem; I thought of the inside of a cloud chamber, marked by a cascade of electrons, freed from their molecule. I thought of all those things, and then I got frightened. I got frightened not just because the work was remarkable, but because the woman I had known ten years before could no more have made it than someone who was deaf, mute, and blind could have described the northern lights. Before Andrea had unfolded the piece on the floor, I had privately granted her the right to have had whatever religious experience she had had, even if it wasn't in English, but just as I had expected to see something like an Oriental madonna sitting inside her cabinet before she opened it, I had also expected to see something as obviously religious as a lotus blossom or a flock of cranes before she'd shown me the photomosaic on the floor. Instead, I'd seen an image of pure energy, as dense and multifaceted as a cubist landscape.

When I asked her what the individual images in the piece were, she smiled at me as if we were a comedy act and I were her straight man. Soon after she had started chanting to the scroll she called her Gohonzon, she said, there had been a flood in her apartment. The water had ruined a pile of eight- by ten-inch Kodalith negatives of her own skin she'd made years before. On impulse, she'd held them up to the light and photographed them as their emulsion ran and peeled and dribbled away. *Like the skin of snakes,* I thought. Then, also on impulse, she said, she'd ordered ten prints of each frame, and when she had them, she began to lay them out in the order she'd shot them. The last print of the last frame she had was the last print she needed to complete the piece on the floor. It happened, she said, like magic, as if the work had made itself. Since by then I knew what I was there for, I asked her what she called the piece. She called it "Diamond Precept." In spite of myself, I asked her what that meant. I asked even though I remembered that in Chinese alchemy the diamond body was a perfect state of internal equilibrium in which a person's energy was detached from all external objects and turned back toward its own center. I asked because I realized that I wasn't leaving until she told me how she'd got from the beginning to the end of her own alphabet in ten years.

It was a longer story than I'd imagined. It started earlier and ran later than I'd thought. It took her three days to tell it, and when it came out, it had as many bits and pieces as one of her mosaics. Parts of it sounded like a fairy tale; parts, like a melodrama. Some of it could have been engraved by William Hogarth, some of it painted by Willem de Kooning or Francis Bacon. Her sound track had everything in it from Smetana and Sibelius to the Velvet Underground and the Talking Heads. At one point she told me she thought she was the reincarnation of Empress Elisabeth of Austria. If I told it the way she did, it would run off the page. The best place to begin is when she was four or five and her school called up her mother and father to ask to see them. Andrea had been given a spatial relations intelligence test and had nearly gone off the scale. She'd taken the test again, but she'd scored just as well the second time. The school wanted to let her parents know that they had a child with an IQ of 180 on their hands. Andrea had known all along that she'd be an artist. By the time she was tested she was trying to copy Gauguins; by the time she was six she'd succeeded. By then she was writing and illustrating her own poems—poems about lovers lying in each other's arms by the sea. While her friends drew stick figures, Andrea rendered her subjects in light and shadow. In the city she made perspective drawings; in the country she sketched landscapes. In school she always got A's, so her mother wanted her to go to Radcliffe, but Andrea knew that she was more an artist than a scholar. When she was sixteen she applied to the Rhode Island School of Design and was accepted. That summer she prepared herself by fasting to become "invulnerably beautiful." By the time she arrived in Providence, she said, she looked like Greta Garbo and talked like Mae West. Six months later she panicked and started stuffing food in plastic bags so she could gorge herself in her room.

Andrea got that way for any number of reasons. Some were as ordinary as a mother who wanted her perfect child to be even happier and more beautiful than she herself had ever been. Some were as unheard-of as a hospital that had mixed her up with another baby and handed her to the wrong woman right after she had been born. And some were as unexpected as a grandfather who fed her not just because he loved her but because his brother had died of starvation. Most of what she told me, though, had to do with her father. She didn't so much talk about him as tell stories about him, stories that sounded like fables and began in "Budapest, that magnificent gray lion, spread out, sprawlingly, across the Danube." The stories she told me were ones she'd heard from people who thought her father was a national hero. Because of everything she'd heard, Andrea believed herself to be the daughter of an exiled political saint. The only trouble with claiming such a lineage is that saints, political or otherwise, seldom make good fathers or even devoted husbands. If their wives and children are lucky, they fill the holes left in their hearts with their consciences. And if, by chance, a man who is a saint is the father of a little girl who scores 180 on a spatial relations test, then the art she's destined to make will have an offering to him hidden in it, an offering that's an act of both redemption and expiation. How Andrea came to make the art she finally made begins with her father. It also ends with a Buddhist monk who may not have been a saint but who was a prophet and a political exile. The monk was Japanese and was born in the thirteenth century; her father was Hungarian and was born just before the First World War. By the time she was thirty she'd joined them to each other, fused them with herself, and encapsulated them in her work.

Andrea's father was a Hungarian states-man, a political theorist, and an author, a man whose name was so common in Hungary that one day it saved his life. From 1939 until 1946 he'd been the leader of the Hungarian Peasant party, a major political party that espoused land redistribution, equality, and national self-determination. He wrote twelve books in his life, three of them novels, one of them, *The Ninety and Nine,* about a priest and a Communist who sit together in a prison cell, arguing with each other until they are both taken out and shot. He was as handsome as he was eloquent, but by the time Andrea was old enough to understand what he could have told her, he'd grown silent. Others told her his story. They said that when the Nazis came for him in Budapest, he escaped by running into a tower. In the tower were a man and his daughter, who hid him. They were aristocrats, the owners of a great country estate, the very sort of people who would have had the most to lose if his party had ever won. The Nazis helped all of them forget their differences. For the rest of the war they hid him. In 1945, as soon as it was safe, he ran for Parliament. Andrea said he looked like a movie star, talked like a poet, and was as solid as an oak. All that won him the chairmanship of a parliamentary committee on land reform. The newspapers called him the Peasant in the Tuxedo. Everyone joked that he'd been elected by the women's vote. Two years later the Communists arrested him as a subversive. He

escaped again and headed for the Austrian border. There the guards asked him if he was *the* Imre Kovács. That was like asking him if he was *the* John Doe. He told them he wasn't, but he'd heard of him, so they let him pass. From Austria, he crossed into Switzerland.

In 1947 everyone who escaped from Hungary immigrated either to Australia or America. In 1949 Kovács chose America: It was free, it was powerful, and it was the best place to go for help against the Soviets. Cold war politics aside, Andrea's story sounded wonderful: First, the Peasant in the Tuxedo is sheltered by Aristocrats in a Tower. Then, at a border crossing, the hero becomes Everyman and No Man, a twentieth-century Ulysses, escaping the Communist Cyclops by lying while he tells the truth. And finally, the Poet becomes the Freedom Fighter, seeking shelter, this time, in the Home of the Brave. It all sounded like something that should have been filmed in Technicolor, but I didn't ask Andrea any questions. All she knew was what she had been told by other people—those who, forty years after her father had fled Hungary, still believed that he was a great hero. Heroes are supposed to follow a script. Even if there wasn't one, all that mattered was that Imre had left Hungary and met Andrea's mother in America; if that hadn't happened, there would have been no Andrea, no pictures, and no story.

The details were that Andrea's father met

Andrea's mother in 1951, in the offices of Radio Free Europe, in the Empire State Building, where he was a writer and she had a summer job. Six months later they were married, and three years after that, when Andrea was two, their marriage fell apart. It fell apart because Imre Kovács was a profoundly solitary man who carried inside him a dream, one that drew women to him as it pulled him away. When Andrea's mother met him, she was a twenty-year-old Radcliffe student, as poor as she was beautiful and as beautiful as she was innocent and gifted. She fell in love with a man who was nearly twice her age and who'd already lost more than she'd ever had. For six months, even a year, he was her Prince in Exile and she was another Princess in a Tower. Together, she thought, they'd found their kingdom. He, of course, had other ideas. There were men he knew, like him, who were planning a revolution in Hungary. When the time came, he'd leave his wife in America and return from exile. When Andrea's mother realized this, she raged at him. One day, Andrea said, when she was very young, she saw her father come out of her mother's room crying. She watched him as he walked down the stairs and wept. She ran to tell her mother something was wrong, but her mother was very angry. She was angry because she couldn't do anything: Imre Kovács was in love, but not with another woman; he had a heart, but he'd left it in another country. By 1955 he'd moved out, and Andrea and

her mother were living with her grandparents. She said she used to stand and stare and long for the light across the street. By the time she was five, she was singing songs to airplanes about her mother and her father who'd gone far away and left her all alone.

In reality, her mother had a part-time job, and her father was living off Riverside Drive, waiting for the revolution. In 1958 Andrea's mother asked her father to marry her again. The revolution had failed. He was still at Radio Free Europe, but he was more alone than ever. Andrea's mother still loved him very much, but all that remained of the Exiled Prince was a stoic who'd survived the death of his own country. His friends were dead; his hope was dead; it took him years to accept the fact that he was still alive. So he remarried Andrea's mother, moved his family into a fine apartment, and then he left, sometimes for as long as six months at a time, on missions to places like Latin America, where he said he served as an American adviser on land reform.

In his absence, Andrea and her mother fell in love. They consoled each other like sisters; they talked and laughed like girl friends. Every morning Andrea massaged her mother's legs; her mother said she had magical hands. Every night her mother helped her with her homework. The arrangement made them both happy, but only for a while. Andrea's mother needed a husband, and Andrea needed a father. Andrea wanted to be perfect to make her mother happy, but even straight A's couldn't absorb all her mother's rage and remorse or all the sorrow and anger mixed up in Andrea's heart. When Andrea's mother was sad, Andrea tried to console her, but when her mother was angry, Andrea had nothing left to give and nowhere to hide. Her father was gone; her mother filled her world. Long ago she'd seen her father leave her mother's room, crying. She was afraid she'd be next. The only place left to go was inward, so she began to build walls around herself. Some kept her anger in and her sorrow out; others kept her guilt away. In between she lived alone and kept watch, afraid of losing and being lost.

The only place she came out was in the country, at her grandfather's summer house. It was a fourteen-room labyrinth that had once been a rest home. Her grandfather had bought it at an auction for next to nothing, and every summer, until Andrea was ten and the highway department destroyed it, she and her mother stayed there. The house was on two acres, bordered by a mountain on one side and the Delaware River on the other. There was a stream full of trout, and dozens of apple and cherry trees whose scents filled the air. At the beginning of every summer, her father came up from the city to help her grandfather prepare the house for the season. He was as happy then as a man who'd been lost and somehow found his way home. Andrea would watch him cut the tall grass with a scythe, as strong and steady and sure as a peasant cutting hay in the Danube Valley. He was so big and powerful that for fun he bought a buggy, and then he pulled Andrea in it, back and forth, up and down the road, like a horse. Sometimes he'd take her under the arms and hurl her up in the air like a rocket. Other times he'd hold her and pull her so that her legs stretched out and she felt as if she were flying. But most of the time he never touched her and never liked to be touched. He'd come and go and walk alone, as tall as a tree, as remote as a walled city.

After another five years there was nothing left of her parents' marriage. Her mother got angrier, and her father grew quieter. Her mother would cry and rage, and her father would turn away. One day, when Andrea was ten, her mother told her she was getting a divorce. Andrea began to laugh and couldn't stop until she started to cry. Months went by. Her mother told her she'd met someone she liked very much. Andrea asked her to promise there wouldn't be any more fights. Her mother promised, and Andrea met the man her mother wanted to marry. He was as outspoken and demonstrative as her father had been silent and withdrawn. Her mother was happier than Andrea had ever seen her, but all Andrea felt was pity for herself and her father: for her father because the new marriage would leave him with neither a family nor a country; for herself because she feared her new father would separate her from her mother. Soon she and Imre both would be exiles.

Once her mother had married again, Andrea saw her father only once a week. On Sundays she'd go to his apartment, and he'd cook one of her favorite dinners, something special, like Hungarian noodles sprinkled with cheese. Then they'd sit and watch television and laugh when he'd try to pronounce something, and Andrea would correct him. When she got sleepy, he'd make her some chocolate milk, and then she'd ask him to carry her into bed. She'd lie there and grow terribly sad; they both were lonely, and there was nothing they could do. He was a man whose life and work inspired a whole generation in exile, but he lived alone. She was his daughter; she could have given him so much, but all they shared were dinner and television. He'd never learned to express his own heart; she didn't know what she could do to console him. Her thoughts made her cry.

Only once a year, during the summer, did they spend more than an evening together. They'd go to Cape Cod, and her father walked the streets of Provincetown until he found a room in a guesthouse. She was a teenager by then and very pretty, and she worried that people might think the wrong thing about the two of them sharing a room. In restaurants her father insisted on having a quiet table, and if people nearby grew noisy, he'd grow offended and start an argument that always embarrassed her. They were happiest when they walked alone to the far dunes, along narrow paths to the empty beaches. Along the way grew wild rose hips, plump, succulent, and bitter little fruits, which they picked and ate. Then they climbed the dunes, and all alone they stood and looked out at the sea, like two solitary figures in a painting. At night they shared some Portuguese tuna and some bread. Then they went down to the wharves, and as the fishermen opened their holds, they smelled the lobsters and the crabs and the sea. They turned and looked at the lights of the little town, and Andrea held her father's hand and told him that it was very hard for her to talk but that she loved him very much.

She applied to the Rhode Island School of Design because she thought it was the art school equivalent of Harvard. Her mother had gone to Radcliffe and reared her on stories of her undergraduate glory. After RISD accepted her, Andrea grew frightened. All the fear and sorrows of a lonely little girl who sang to airplanes returned. In her own defense, she decided to turn herself into an effigy so beautiful that no one would ever approach it or, if anyone did, would never guess who was hiding inside. That summer, while her mother and stepfather vacationed in Europe, she lived with her grandparents and fasted. In the fall she arrived at school, looking as elegant as an Egyptian cat and talking as suggestively and cynically as a world-weary artist. Since her fellow students were more inexperienced than she'd anticipated, her effigy didn't have the effect she'd imagined. The women who might have been her friends were repelled, but everyone else was drawn to it. Homosexuals in fashion design begged her to be their model; lesbians kept watch by her bed when she caught the flu; and heterosexual men, aware of her tender age, debated the penalties and possibilities of a charge of statutory rape. Eight weeks of not eating had sharpened her appetite not just for food but for all the solace and comfort that came with it. Instead, she provoked only a predatory attention that frightened her and drove her deeper inside. Man after man tried to sleep with her, but in spite of the way she talked, she remained a virgin who insisted on wearing her pantyhose to bed and then, in the morning, rushed back to her dormitory to console herself with a half dozen ice cream bars.

Her inexperience notwithstanding, she produced art that was as elegant and accomplished as she looked. In response to an assignment to build a time machine by the next class, she mixed oil, water, and mercury and sealed the solution between two pieces of Plexiglas. No sooner would her instructors pose a problem than she'd arrive at a solution and execute it so inventively that their exchanges became as rapid as volleys across a net. There was one exercise they gave her, though, that she said made her pause. They called it a hypercube; its intent was to trace the movement of a two-dimensional cube over time and space. As Andrea described it, a cube was drawn in perspective, and then it was redrawn slightly above and to the right of itself on the picture plane. After that, she said, connecting lines were drawn between each vertex of the first cube and each vertex of the second. Once she had made her first hypercube, she said, she kept on making them, over and over again. Ten years later she still thought about the exercise. She even thought it had affected "Diamond Precept." From the way she described it, though, I couldn't understand it; it seemed too simple and dry. Why had it fascinated her then, and how had it lasted so long? I asked her to draw it, and when she did, I understood. At first, the connecting lines appeared to do nothing but trace the cube's movement from one position to the other. But after that first glance a whole new set of cubes, aligned along an axis other than the first, emerged. Another glance revealed another pattern; one realignment followed the next, nearly as rapidly as I blinked until, at last, I saw that the web of lines formed a cross inside an octagon. Her instructors had spoken of the hypercube as if it were just an art school exercise. In fact, what they had given to their students to draw was something that Tibetan Buddhists called a yantra, a complex, symmetrical pattern that was a type of mandala used by novitiates to focus their minds during the early stages of meditation. Thirty years ago Carl Jung first described such patterns, executed by people who had never practiced Buddhism or traveled to Tibet. He spoke of mandalas as images made in conditions of psychic dissociation or disorientation "in an attempt at self-healing." Ten years before Andrea had ever chanted a mantra and then made a piece full of gemlike hexagons, she had copied and recopied a graphic device that had been used for thousands of years to calm and center the mind.

In spite of the hypercube, she began to lose control of herself. She ate and ate and ate and couldn't stop. The food always calmed and quieted her but never for long. As she ate, her mask sank into her flesh until she looked like a seventeen-year-old fat girl. At the end of her first year she moved out of her dormitory and into a house that Rhode Island had labeled historic. Such houses could never be torn down, but they could be moved; this one had been jacked up and plopped down on top of a clothing store. Its stairs were dark and broken and led up to a suite of rather dirty little rooms. Andrea lived in one, next to six others, all inhabited by members of a rock and roll band called The Motels. Once they had all been RISD students, but they'd never left after graduation. Instead, they started wearing a lot of leopardskin and singing songs like "Mother-in-law" and "Christmas in Japan in July," all with a Motown sound. Their lead was a huge, fat man named Ruddy Cheeks; their chorus line called itself the Tampoons. Andrea started to wear black and follow them around. She was still a virgin, but she was

so overweight that few paid attention to her, and only then because she talked as entertainingly as a freak in a sideshow. During her second year she studied architecture and kept watch for someone to rid her of her hymen. Eventually she chose a fellow student. One night she knocked on his door and told him she wanted to be deflowered. He confessed that he'd never been the first in line before, but he did have a pamphlet that explained how to go about it. While he read its step-by-step directions, he obliged her. When it was over and she started talking to him, he told her to stop babbling like a teenager. She went back to her room, bleeding, lonely, and frigid.

She kept making art, but she used it as an effigy. Her life was unpredictable and confused; its primary emotion was pain, but her art was cool, cerebral, ironic, and self-assured. In her third year she studied sculpture and executed two pieces made of components she arranged and rearranged and then photographed. For the first, she cast 100 lead ingots that she discovered, to her delight, looked like cobblestones. She lugged them outside, laid them on the street, and photographed the irony. Then she hauled them back in, dumped a mound of dirt on the foundry floor, paved it with her ingots, and walked across in triumph. All the while she photographed the performance. After that she began to collect burned-out long neon tubes. When she had fifty or sixty, she began to lay them here and there in patterns like so many fragile and potentially lethal pickup sticks. She'd lay them in a row under a bridge or in a line along a wall and then photograph them. Finally, she stood them on end, leaning one against, but slightly out of line with, the other until they formed a complex curve called a hyperbolic paraboloid, which she had studied in architecture. At last, when the tubes slipped and shattered and released their gas, her photographs became not just a record but the very piece itself.

Her life and her art could have continued their separate trajectories if she hadn't seen the work of Dennis Oppenheim and Vito Acconci, men who restored the artist and his life to their art. In one work, Oppenheim took the last scribbled mark his father made before he died and transformed it into a pattern of light made by burning flares on a ten-acre hillside. In another, Acconci lay naked and blindfolded on a small circular dais. An audience surrounded him and watched as he pulled himself around in a circle on his belly with one hand behind his back until he reached the end of his strength. Then he blindly stabbed out his hand and screamed, "You! I'm pointing at you! Your time's up! You're gonna die! I want you to die!" After that he caught his breath and started pulling himself around again until he grew exhausted, stabbed out his hand, and declared another death.

Both Acconci and Oppenheim performed such rituals, some sweet, some harrowing, but all using their bodies, their words, their gestures, their very lives to enact and reveal a variety of hidden truths about themselves and their audience. Encouraged by their example, Andrea began to make slides of her own unhappy face. One night she projected a slide of her eyes into the corner of her room; the way they split on the wall made her think of the splits in her life. Then, without understanding why, she felt herself drawn into them along the light of the projector as if she were a plane on a glide path or Narcissus bending down into the pool. She said it was the first time she'd ever seen a picture of her own feelings. She changed her major from sculpture to photography and spent her last year at RISD projecting slides of her face onto everything and then photographing the results. She called them her Rorschachs, studied them as if they were, and then printed them at four by six feet. When she exhibited them at the end of the year, she called the show "Laughing and Screaming in a Vacuum." She felt as if her life had gushed out onto the walls. She knew she was making art as therapy, but she had no choice. Her life and her art had collided, and though she was ashamed of how lonely and hungry she was, the projected self-portraits were her way of acknowledging the pain and confessing it to others. Those others sometimes chose to ignore what they saw: Aaron Siskind, the master photographer who was one of her teachers, talked about her images as abstractions rather than egomaniacal contortions. He said she had the perfect face, since it was as flat and white as a movie screen. With that, Andrea was graduated from RISD and applied to Yale.

She said she was accepted there because the faculty who interviewed her were relieved to find someone as unhappy in public as they were in private. For the next two years she associated with painters and swung back and forth between fasting, followed by gaiety, and eating herself into a stupor, followed by despair. The best friend she had was Marjorie, who fasted and ate as compulsively as she did. Most people thought she and Andrea were lovers, but the only secret they shared was food. Andrea would withdraw to her apartment and its empty refrigerator and stay in bed until she lost weight. Then she'd come out and talk and drink and laugh and make nasty remarks about such things as traditional photography. Sooner or later she'd get carried away and gorge herself and then disappear like Cinderella at midnight. That cycle went on until she spread herself all over the walls of the school's art gallery.

The only interruption came during the summer of her first year at Yale when she went to New York and fell in love. It happened while she was visiting a painter named Jaime. Everyone from RISD always stopped to see Jaime because he was always home. Jaime never, ever left his loft. Once, before he was a painter, Jaime had been in the navy, on board a submarine. Toward the end of a long voyage he'd been ordered to clean up behind a boiler, but he was too big to fit. He'd had to choose beween burning and disobedience, so he went into a trance. When he came out, the navy discharged him with plenty of medical benefits. As a result, Jaime painted all day with a decent pension. The afternoon Andrea walked in, there was someone under his table, kicking and clawing his way into the center of a hollow log. Andrea was attracted to whoever it was at once. Jaime said he was an out-of-work RISD dropout who slept on his kitchen floor. Andrea found out his name was David Byrne, but she was too shy to say anything. Then late one night, when everyone was sitting in the dark listening to a recording of the Velvet Underground, Andrea sent Byrne a note about the music; soon after that they were lovers. During the day they'd sit outside Jaime's place on the Bowery and drink wine, or they'd run across the street to a bar called CBGB's that had pool tables and live music. Onstage, people like Debbie Harry were trying to sing their way to stardom while no one listened. Byrne wanted to discover how to turn his life into an art project. He kept talking about some sort of sacrifice, like becoming a computer programmer but never telling anyone his true mission. He even talked about becoming a rock and roll star. Andrea encouraged him. She thought he was a genius; they spent days together planning his future. The main problem was that he was broke and she had to go back to Yale. Before she left, she convinced him to take a job as a movie usher. He came up to see her a few months later, but he was so ragged and desperate that she told him to go home. He didn't come again until she invited him and his record collection to her opening.

After she had been graduated, she moved to New York, and she and Byrne traded places. She wasn't sleeping on anyone's floor, but all she had was a box of blowups and the blessings of Henry Geldzahler. She took her portfolio to the Metropolitan and showed it to the curator of contemporary art. He looked at it, said it was the strongest student work he'd ever seen, and told her to come back in five years. By then she was afraid she'd be dead and David Byrne would be famous. Byrne had already hit bottom and was coming up fast, playing all the clubs. Andrea put on her black leather jacket, her tight black pants, her high-heeled black leather boots, and her Liz Taylor—Cleopatra look-alike eye makeup, and she made an appointment with the curator of the hippest commercial gallery in the city. When she walked in, the poor man was smitten by a vision of his very own superstar. Edie Sedgwick had long ago turned into a piece of coal, and Andy Warhol had just gotten a bellyful of surgical scars. Andrea looked like a New Discovery. When she showed him her slides, the man fell in love. He even convinced the owner of the gallery, a man of wealth and taste, to come to her loft to see the real thing. The owner stood there and looked at all her scratched skin, billowing flesh, black fingernails, and sleeping lovers, and he made her a promise. He chose his words with great care. "I will try," he said, "to find a place in art history for your eccentric medium." It was the last thing he said to her for the next ten years. A few weeks later Byrne told her to get a job. All she had were problems; what she needed was work. If he could start as an usher, so could she.

Since she wasn't crazy about the movies, she tried the record stores. The first place that had an opening was called Tracks. It sold the music and memorabilia of dead rock and roll stars. The tapes and records were all bootlegs from Winston-Salem. All the personally autographed pictures of John Lennon, Jimi Hendrix, and Jim Morrison were carefully signed by Arnie, the owner, in the back room. Andrea brought her résumé along, but Arnie's idea of a job interview was a quick feel in his Eldorado. After that he offered her a job. Since Andrea hardly felt anything anyway, she accepted. It only confirmed her worst suspicions. The next day she started selling original silk scarves Elvis had worn at his last concert—they were made of rayon and came in cartons of 500 from Hong Kong. After a few months Arnie took her aside and broke the bad news: She wasn't making the sales, so she'd have to go. Unless, of course, she wanted to do him a little favor after work. Andrea didn't have any money, so she didn't have any choice. She also didn't care; by then Byrne had left her. All she had was Arnie and Tracks and the art she'd begun to make like someone playing solitaire with a magic deck.

Just before she'd left Yale, she'd switched from color Polaroids to 35 mm. She'd shoot a roll as if it were an exercise in automatic writing, then take the film to a drugstore. She'd order three- by five-inch prints of everything, specify a glossy finish, and let the processing machines make the rest of the decisions for her. Whatever pictures came back in the envelope made her feel like an amnesiac who'd just found part of her diary floating in a bottle. She knew that each picture, each sequence, each roll referred to herself, but what was revealed was a puzzle she put aside until, over time, the envelopes from the drugstore began to accumulate. Then she'd open the envelopes and begin to deal out the pictures as if they were cards from a deck and she were telling her fortune.

The first time she did that was just before she and Arnie had their job interview. Some of the pictures were from New Haven, but most were from the time between her show at Yale and her first day at Tracks. On top of the pile were pictures she'd made of Marjorie, her girl friend and double. They were mauve-toned, underexposed nudes on a bed, in a light so dim and dreamy that the grain of the film covered her like a mist. These Andrea laid out in a solid square. In the next envelope were pictures she'd made of her own thighs and vagina, and in the next were fleshy nudes she'd made of herself seen from above. Around the square she'd made of Marjorie, she began to build a spiral. For two circuits, it was composed of pictures of herself, but then it changed, just as the pictures in the pile changed to close-ups of a fish head that, from below, looked exactly like the genitals of a dead woman. These continued for half a circuit, then changed again, and the spiral ended with bloody pictures she'd made of her legs after she'd cut them while shaving in the bath. To her surprise, the last picture she had in her hand was also the last picture she needed to complete the spiral. When she stepped back, she saw what she'd done: Without consciously knowing it, she'd made a mandala or, as she called it, "an iconic image," nearly four feet square. At its center, like the target of a bull's-eye, was a romantic softness; all around it spiraled allusions to feminine shape, odor, frigidity, and blood. Every picture in it she made on impulse, generated by her unconscious, like a surrealist experimenting with automatic writing. She'd made what she called "an object of contemplation," which revealed more to her about her own sex and sexuality than anything she'd ever done. She felt as if the work had made itself and used her as its agent. She called the work "Bouillabaisse." As her life broke apart, she began to make more mandalas from the pieces. She called them photomosaics and interpreted them like dreams. One had ninety-nine images at its center, so she named it "The Enigmatic

Ninety and Nine" in honor of her father's novel about the Communist and the priest. One, called "Surrogate Love," and another, called "The Red Eye of Love," were summaries of what had happened between Byrne and her. Some were rectangles with cool blue centers; others were radiant red parallelograms; one was six feet long and eight feet high and had 400 images in it.

Most of the money she made at Tracks went to either the photofinisher or the grocer. Her hunger never left her. Sometimes she spent more money on food than on film; sometimes she took pictures as ravenously as she ate. Finally, she couldn't afford her loft anymore and moved into the apartment on Eighth Street. With that she quit her job, declared herself a free-lance fashion photographer, and started talking to the people who lived on the street outside her front door. All of them were castaways, washed up from the sixties. Some were sweet but damaged innocents, some were megalomaniacal speed freaks. All had heroic dreams of their own stardom that reminded her of the stories Byrne used to tell. Byrne's rock and roll dreams had since come true, but Andrea remembered when he had been nothing but a ragged guy with burning eyes who crawled into hollow logs. Byrne had made it, but Andrea was still waiting. She was the child of an exiled hero; she had a Master of Fine Arts degree from Yale, but all she'd done for two years was sell bootleg music and do little favors for a fat man with a hair weave. She began

looking for a dreamer and a martyr to keep her company, but all she found on the street was a guy named Blue Bird and another named Billy Snow.

Blue Bird was kind. He had the body of a dancer and the face of St. Sebastian. Salvador Dali had used him as a model, but too many acid trips had bruised his brain, so he spoke in blank verse that made him hard to understand. He and Andrea became lovers and spent their nights in a room in the Monterey Hotel, taking speed cut with acid that made her dream while it took her hunger away. Andrea knew Billy Snow wasn't nearly as nice, so she never slept with him. He was a speed freak with the face of a rat who hung weights from his penis at night to make it grow. All he talked about, hour after hour, was the musical he was planning to write about himself. He said he was going to produce and direct it, too, but he couldn't decide if he should star in it or not. Andrea kept listening, thinking she was going to write a book about it all called *Birds of Paradise*. They'd walk around together—Billy with his eyes like pinheads, wired from all the speed, and Andrea, numb and gay from plenty of wine. One night she ran into the middle of Houston Street and lay down and waited to get run over. Another night a black limousine pulled up, and a charming man with a Middle Eastern accent invited the two of them to a birthday party. Billy said it was his birthday, too, so he climbed in, pulled Andrea after him, and the limo sped off to a belly-dancing club. Andrea was drunk already, but the men at the table insisted she have more to celebrate. When the club closed, they assured her they'd take her home. Instead, they took her and Billy to a place in the Bronx, where they raped her while Billy sat in the kitchen and played cards.

There'd be days when she'd stay drunk or when she'd eat and couldn't stop. All she had left was her art, but that only chronicled her descent. She made a piece, then, of a man and a woman, their legs intertwined, their bodies cut off below the waist or sliced down the center. The woman was an artist Andrea had known at Yale; the man was none other than Billy Snow. Billy gladly took off his clothes for the occasion, but the woman was modest and insisted on wearing a slip. Andrea photographed them in poses that implied movement, using outdoor film under incandescent light so that, in spite of the woman's reticence, their bodies glowed red in images that looked like frames from a pornographic film. Andrea arranged the prints in a way she'd never done: Instead of laying them side by side, edge to edge, building a mandala from the center out, or the outside in, she took four prints at a time and arranged them in a swastika pattern around an interior hollow square. Each pattern of four images swirling around their empty center became a single unit that Andrea added, one next to the other, seven across and seven down, to form a five-foot square. Beside the whirl-

ing, glowing nudes were black-and-white pictures of Billy alone, as well as of chunks of dead gray concrete and of light falling across the stripes of a tigerskin shirt. Animate and inanimate, human and inhuman, the images swirled in tiny vortices, each around its own emptiness, the whole piece a locked symmetry with no center of its own. When she finished it, Andrea understood what she'd done: Instead of a mandala, she'd made a maelstrom. "I had no gyroscope; I had no center. Until then I'd retained a center and so had the work, but I no longer had a stabilizer. My life was shooting off in all directions; I couldn't synthesize the whole except by throwing people together in a piece. It was a sign of the total fragmentation of my mind and my life."

Her free-lance work barely kept her alive. She'd take her portfolio to different talent and modeling agencies, hoping for assignments to photograph their clients, but no one there had ever heard of Ellsworth Kelly or Henry Geldzahler. One day she went to a talent agency that wasn't interested but that sent her across the hall to one that might be. Sitting behind the desk was what others might have seen to be a typically well-groomed, well-dressed, well-to-do New York professional woman, but to Andrea, in her desperation, she looked like everything she wanted to be and wasn't. The woman's dark hair coiled around her hard, beautiful face as if it were alive; her eyes were like dark gemstones; her skin was perfect. She wore gold and was dressed in a suit trimmed with red fox. Andrea showed her work and then waited for the inevitable. Instead, the woman told her it was wonderful. She spoke with a voice of such resonance and warmth that Andrea nearly cried. She began to ask Andrea questions about herself, and, at first, Andrea answered, but then she began to confess: She was broke and lonely, and even worse, she couldn't stop eating; she'd tried everything, but she always felt as if she were starving. Andrea had never told that to anyone but Marjorie before, as if her eating were a loathsome addiction whose confession would send her to a colony for the insane. Andrea waited for the woman to look disgusted, but instead, she said, "Why don't you try chanting?" Andrea asked, "What?" and the woman said, "Nam-myoho-renge-kyo." It wasn't the first time Andrea had heard it. A stock clerk at Tracks had once asked her if she wanted to try it, but he'd made it sound like having a drink after work, and at that point in Andrea's New York career, she still thought of herself as a Yale graduate who might have suffered a job interview with Arnie but who neither chanted nonsense nor associated with anyone who worked in a warehouse. Times had changed, and the woman behind the desk didn't look like a clerk, so Andrea asked another question: Was chanting like praying to some God? No, said the woman, it was like praying to yourself. People always asked for things when they chanted, she said, but when they got them, it wasn't as if someone in heaven had done them a favor. Andrea began another question, but the woman quieted her. The best thing was to come and chant. The woman gave her an address, and Andrea promised to be there.

The place was a three-room apartment on the Upper West Side, packed with people with no shoes, kneeling thigh to thigh, rolling prayer beads around, and chanting so rapidly that Andrea thought they sounded like crickets from another planet. Andrea waded through them to a spot beside the woman from the agency. She gave Andrea a wonderful smile, then went on chanting, but she encouraged her with her eyes. Andrea cringed. There were too many people; they were too close together; they were too loud; they had holes in their socks. Andrea wanted to leave, but the woman kept smiling at her, so she tried to stumble through the words. Finally, she caught the rhythm and joined the chanting. Once she had, she felt something pop in her like a membrane breaking, and she started to smile. She chanted and chanted, and when she left, she felt as if she'd gone through the sound barrier. "The fortress I'd built and built around my heart cracked open; the little girl trapped in there with all her hope and all her love started to come out."

One meeting didn't do it, though. Andrea went back to her place on Eighth Street, feeling no more or less pleased with herself than if she'd started on a brown rice miracle diet or just attended her first jazzercise class. Her hunger returned; she started drinking again; she was as broke and lonely as ever. One day in a rage she threw her record player against the wall, but that didn't help either. The rent was due, she still felt as if she were starving, and all she had was $20. She got dressed and went to see Arnie at Tracks to ask for her job back. Arnie said he had to be somewhere in five minutes, but she could ride along if she liked. They ended up down by the docks. Arnie wanted another interview. Andrea jumped out of the car with her blouse open and ran. She ran all the way home, locked the door, and knelt in the corner. She felt as if she were falling and drowning at the same time. She put her hands together and started chanting to save her life.

At this point, as Andrea told it, I would have expected to see the snow stop falling onstage while behind her an illuminated scrim revealed a church window and the theater filled with the sound of perfect voices singing the Lord's Prayer. At the last note the footlights would fade, and the curtains would close with the penitent, her back to the audience, staring up at the window, which would have become a blaze of light. People's lives turned to stories sound most convincing when they resemble the narrative forms of their age. Andrea's had begun to sound like a melodrama in which the fallen heroine rises from the gutter, clasps Christ to her heart, and is saved. In some versions the heroine dies after that

and is reborn, a pure soul in Glory. In this part of the century she simply dies, but not before she has suffered in this life all the torments of hell. What happened to Andrea, instead, was that she remembered what the woman at the agency had told her: People who chanted for things often got them. Andrea knew where she was headed: She'd failed her father and her mother and every one of her teachers and friends. She wasn't famous or even a martyr. She was fat, drunk, and unknown; she was living along a sewer, and she'd done it all to herself. She understood all that, but then, instead of taking vows, or dying to be reborn, or just dying, she did what any half-Jewish, half-Hungarian art school graduate living in New York would have done while chanting a Buddhist mantra in transliterated Chinese: She chanted for a good job. It might have been better for the story if she'd chanted and asked to be forgiven or chanted for enlightenment. All that came later. In the beginning, though, her chanting had to do with survival, physical and emotional. By the time I'd met her and heard the whole story, she'd been a Nichiren Shoshu Buddhist for five years, but at first, she knew little, understood less, and chanted the way poor and desperate people pray to Jesus to get what they need and then what they want. No one's ever been able to do without loaves and fishes.

The peculiar thing was that a day after she had chanted for a job, she got one as a teacher of photography, and a week after she had chanted for a show at a gallery, she took her work first to one and then to another, and both promised her exhibitions. Perhaps she should have done these things earlier or, if not done them, then at least have put herself in a position so that they could have happened to her. David Byrne may have started as an usher, and Vincent van Gogh may have lost an ear, but Andrea didn't have to begin her career by working for Arnie. Why she got the teaching job and the promise of gallery shows has any number of explanations. Andrea later spoke of the chanting as if it were a magnet that had realigned the forces of her life in relation to those of the universe. Others might dismiss what happened as luck; someone like Carl Jung would have called it an example of synchronous coincidence, similar to a starving man's finding a quarter on a street or a photographer's always finding himself at the intersection of events that he recognizes as emblems of his own predicament. Whatever the explanation, the chanting at first calmed and centered Andrea, and the coincidences that followed converted her.

The Buddhism Andrea practiced was not precisely the one formulated by the disciples of Siddhartha Gautama 100 years after he died. It was, in fact, an interpretation of an interpretation that had made its way from India to China, from China to Korea, and from Korea to Japan over a period of 1,000 years. The Lotus Sutra that Korean monks brought to Japan in the seventh century A.D. was a text of Chinese rather than Indian origin. In China its parables, miracles, and revelations had inspired several centuries of high art; in Japan ceremonies derived from it were used to alleviate famines, droughts, and epidemics. By the thirteenth century a monastery, initially founded to promulgate the sutra's text and teachings, had grown to an institution of 3,000 buildings and 30,000 monks. An obscure monk who had studied there, a fisherman's son named Nichiren Daishonin, was the founder of the sect whose chanting saved Andrea's life. Nichiren believed himself to be a prophet and saint, a bodhisattva of perseverance foretold in the sutra itself. At the time he proclaimed himself and his doctrine, Japan was in turmoil and danger, threatened by Mongols, racked by insurrection and poverty. Nichiren believed the nation was suffering because its people and rulers had abandoned the Lotus Sutra. The warrior class practiced Zen; the aristocrats indulged in spells; the common people recited mantras to a Buddha of Salvation in the hope of being reborn in a heavenly land to the west. Instead of prayers, sorcery, and meditation, Nichiren preached recitation of a mantra in praise of the Lotus Sutra. If everyone chanted it, he claimed, not only would the nation be saved, but Japan would become a heaven on earth where people no longer believed death was their only salvation. Like Luther, he demanded a return to a primary sacred text, and like Luther, he was prosecuted by the authorities. Twice he was nearly executed; once he was exiled.

Andrea eventually fused Nichiren's struggles, persecution, and exile with those of her father, but the Lotus Sutra itself changed her life and then her art. Its flower was a symbol of redemption and of the simultaneity of cause and effect: Out of the mud grew a pure blossom that was both an end and a beginning, a flower as well as a seedpod. Chinese commentaries on the sutra elaborated ten worlds or states of being that, like the lotus flower and its seeds, existed in the same instant; each of the ten was a more spiritually refined state of being than the next, but each was inherent in the other, and all were simultaneously present, from one moment to the next, in both the universe and the life of every living being. The lowest world, said the commentaries, was hell; next came hunger, animality, anger. Since Andrea had come to New York, she'd inhabited all of them. Then came tranquillity, rapture, learning, realization, inspiration, and, finally, enlightenment. Just as the lotus grew from the mud and just as its blossoms contained its seeds, so every life, no matter how depraved, contained in the midst of its depravity its own enlightenment. The forces within every life and the laws that governed every life were identical to the most powerful forces and laws in the uni-

verse. To chant the mantra in praise of the Lotus Sutra, said Nichiren, was to do three things: The first was to achieve a state of enlightenment; the second was to activate the energies, profound, powerful, and compassionate, inherent in that state of being; the third was to align these energies with those of the universe. Neither Nichiren nor the Chinese before him believed a god presided over any of this. Only human life and the universe had existed from all time and would exist to all eternity. The only thing that prevented human beings from becoming enlightened and from using that energy in congruence with the universe was themselves. If they only chanted the mantra in praise of the Lotus Sutra, said Nichiren, they all would become Buddhas, not after an endless series of deaths and rebirths but within their own lifetimes as they lived and breathed.

Andrea felt as if she'd drilled a freshwater well into the center of her life. She'd never believed she had the patience or the confidence or the kindness necessary to teach, but at the end of her first semester her students thanked her. Without knowing it, she'd done something she hadn't since she was a little girl: She'd given more than she'd taken. A center returned to her art, again, but its content changed. Soon after she'd started chanting, she made a piece called "Tribal Gifts," a vertical triptych, twelve feet high and five feet wide, composed of 500 images that paid homage to the people she'd loved and the love they'd given her. At the center of one panel was a rectangle of twelve images that alluded to Jaime, the painter, to whose loft she'd returned again and again, long after she and David Byrne had met and then parted. For years Jaime had been a video artist as well as a painter, who incorporated his friends and himself in his tapes. Often he'd turned his camera on Andrea and allowed her to act out her fears and fantasies and then to see them replayed. She had used Jaime's tapes as she used her own art; in tribute to him she held up her hand and photographed it against a latticework window shade whose backlit slats resembled, in her pictures, a video screen composed of alternating lines of light and shadow. In the center of the second panel, she paid homage to Marjorie, her closest friend at Yale, by photographing the hair of a blonde, sensually intertwined with hair as black as her own. In the center of the third panel were close-ups of a good-luck cactus that, instead of trouble, Andrea had just given to herself. Encasing these solid central rectangles were alternating rows and blocks of images of three objects, photographed at close range. One set consisted of close-ups of the rainbow-hued fringes of a Hungarian silk scarf, another set was of the convoluted pink flesh of a kidney, and the third was of a strand of pearls coiled across and strung through the glistening nodes of that organ. The Hungarian scarf alluded to her father's nationality, which was her heritage; the pearls were a gift he'd once given her; the kidney was an ingredient in a dish he'd often cooked for her. In the triptych the pearls became symbols of spirit; the kidneys, of flesh and appetite. For the first time they were intertwined. Until "Tribal Gifts," most of her pieces had been equivalent to screams. From then on they became celebrations.

Soon after "Tribal Gifts," she requested and received the scroll I'd seen hanging in the black lacquer cabinet when I'd first come to visit. This scroll, or Gohonzon, was a facsimile of one inscribed by the current high priest of the Nichiren Shoshu sect, but even that was only a copy executed by the high priest of the one originally inscribed by Nichiren himself before his death. Down the center of the scroll Nichiren, a master calligrapher, had written, in Chinese, the words of his mantra; along its borders he had inscribed the ideograms of the ten worlds or states of being; in the upper and lower corners of the scroll he had written the names of those who had participated in one of the more miraculous parables in the Lotus Sutra, the parable of the treasure tower. In that parable an immense jeweled stupa, or treasure tower, had appeared in midair above the mountain peak where Siddhartha Gautama, now called Sakyamuni, sat surrounded by a vast crowd of disciples, priests, nuns, and onlookers. First, out of the tower had come a voice praising Sakyamuni and his teachings. Then the tower had opened to reveal a

Buddha who had achieved enlightenment and died aeons before Sakyamuni had been born. This ancient Buddha then invited Sakyamuni to rise and sit, as an equal, beside him. Commentators had always interpreted the treasure tower as a symbol of the self, and the union of the two Buddhas as a conjunction of objective and subjective wisdom, but Nichiren's disciples had extended the metaphor. The entire scroll, executed and signed by Nichiren, was a symbol of the union of the self with the basic laws of the universe. It was that and more: The entire scroll was Nichiren's psychic equivalent, the very fingerprint of his enlightened consciousness, a map made of and by his life's energy. To study it and to chant it were not only to awaken that consciousness but also to activate the enlightened energy in all who looked while they chanted. The scroll was a more powerful religious instrument than any mantra or hypercube Andrea had ever studied, in or out of art school. Its effect on the walls she'd built around her anger and fear since she was a child was slow and steady, but its effect on her art was dramatic.

One of the galleries that had reviewed her portfolio had promised her a show in December. Her opening was only a few months away when the pipes in her apartment burst, the Kodaliths she had made, long ago, of her skin were ruined, and on impulse, she'd photographed their emulsions peeling away. She knew she wanted to make a piece that would represent the way both she and her art were shedding their old skins, but she wasn't sure how. For an hour or even two hours every day she chanted in front of her Gohonzon, and then, refreshed, she returned to work on the piece she was trying to construct. Days of chanting and working went by. Eventually the solution came, and, as before, the last print she had in her hand was the last print she needed. All that was familiar, but she was startled by the way the diamond shapes had entered the piece. It wasn't simply that she'd been too close as she'd worked to see them emerge; even when she'd drawn back, she couldn't, at first, comprehend their origin. When she at last understood, she was amazed: They had come from the Gohonzon itself. The scroll's calligraphy, down its center, along its borders, and in its corners, filled it in such a way that out of the white mass of paper and the black mass of the calligraphy a subtle six-sided shape emerged. To chant while looking at the Gohonzon was called the Diamond Precept, but the scroll itself had hidden in it a diamond shape, a shape originally delineated by the strokes of Nichiren's brush and then copied and recopied hundreds of times by hundreds of high priests since the thirteenth century. The shape was a metaphor composed of precepts, but like a work of art, it was also a psychic fingerprint of its creator. Without consciously knowing it, Andrea had been imprinted with a pattern of energy, and then, knowing it but not knowing it, like a surrealist, she had transferred and transformed that imprint in the process of her art.

All this time her hunger had grown steadily worse. Day after day she chanted to overcome it until, one morning, it left her. She noticed it the same way someone who has lived for years with the sounds of the city notices silence the first day in the mountains. Perhaps her hunger hadn't disappeared; perhaps it had only changed. Instead of an appetite for food, Andrea believed it had become an appetite for enlightenment. Or perhaps chanting had replaced eating. Whatever happened, she decided to live with herself: overweight and frigid but no longer hungry. Her show had gotten good reviews. She went out for breakfast and sat at the counter. While she waited for her order, she read a book about Buddhism. During Nichiren's life he had fought with other Buddhists, and after his death his disciples had fought with each other. Nichiren Shoshu, Andrea's sect, called its practice the True Buddhism. During the Second World War its leaders had refused to cooperate with the fascists. Some had died in prison; some had been broken and collaborated; one alone had refused and survived. Kept in solitary confinement until the end, he stayed alive by chanting. It was said he repeated the mantra two billion times. As Andrea read, she felt the eyes of the man beside her. She turned and asked if he'd ever heard of the True Buddhism; at the same moment he asked her if

she'd ever chanted. They both laughed. He asked if she'd done her morning gongyo; then she asked if he had. They discovered it was too early for both of them. When they finished breakfast, Andrea invited him to her apartment. After they chanted, they talked. Andrea confessed she needed help to feel things. That's when he told her he was a locksmith. They both smiled. Andrea told him she'd been looking for someone to open her heart. He said he thought he could help. After a few weeks he found the key. That's when she realized he looked exactly like her father.

That's also when she realized the connection among her father, Nichiren, and herself. Both men had tried to make revolutions; both had suffered persecution and exile for their beliefs. Her father had devoted his life to the freedom of his country. For forty years he'd struggled for economic and social justice and self-determination, but Hungary remained occupied and he remained trapped within himself. Nichiren had preached the potential enlightenment of all human beings, the clarification of all human consciousness, the potential Buddhahood of every inhabitant of the earth. Her father's revolution had been political and economic, but its failure had shattered him and his country. Nichiren's revolution had been religious, and 700 years after his death, it had spread to America and saved Andrea's life. Her father had brought her into the world and inspired her with noble ideals, but he was a solitary man who talked eloquently of self-determination yet had never learned to express his own heart. Nichiren's Buddhism had gone beyond ideology to enlightenment. Instead of a revolution of ways and means, it spoke of a revolution of consciousness that spread from the inside out. It claimed that any person who achieved enlightenment lived in peace and did justice. If all people achieved enlightenment, then earth would become heaven. Andrea decided to serve that goal with her art. She may not have invented the visual syntax of the photomosaic, but she had extended it. She could use it now to chronicle her efforts to live in harmony with the universe. She could record her own ascent and, by recording it, she could encourage others. Instead of an art of pain and denial, she could perfect an art of hope.

She got her first chance to try when the New Museum invited her to be in a group show. One afternoon she was lying in the sun on the roof of her building, chewing a carrot. When she stood up, she tipped over a bottle of lotion. She watched it spread across a patch of tar that had bubbled in the sun. Clear, bright little highlights glistened like tiny stars. She looked closer and thought she saw a galaxy. She picked up her camera, knelt, and began to make pictures. She stood and bit off some pieces of carrot and spit them into the oil. She took off her gold necklace and threw it down onto the tar. She had some prayer beads and wound them down in coils onto the roof. She photographed them all: the bub-

bles, the tar, the oil, the carrots that looked like sunbursts, the round white beads, and the long gold chains. Then she looked up and saw the adjoining wall of a building that had been painted black. It was as tall as she was and more than twenty feet long. That would be the size of her piece. She ordered twenty-five prints of every frame and when she had them, she began to lay them out in blocks of five, each block a solid square of twenty-five images, thirty-six blocks in all. The solution was handsome, but it was a design without velocity.

Seven days before the opening she tore the piece apart and began again. She worked and chanted; chanted, then worked. She saw that if some of the pictures were laid out, each one above but slightly to the left of the other, they formed an orange streak that tumbled like a comet from the upper right to the lower left. Others looked like showers of light. Still others had loops and spirals that rolled from frame to frame like the pulse of a wave that bounded and rebounded from one end of the piece to the other. All that remained in her hand were one set of pictures of the tar bubbles and another of the strands of her necklace. From the tar she built a tall window in space and framed it with the gold strands of her necklace, which looked to her like "Einsteinian markings on a blackboard." The wave form that pulsed from right to left across the center of the piece seemed to enter the window and come rolling out the other side.

She knew the piece was finished because she had nothing left in her hands. She backed away to look and thought at once of what had happened to Nichiren: He had said too much, made too many claims, offended too many powerful people, so the soldiers had come and carried him off to his execution. They took him down to a place by the sea called Tatsunokuchi Beach, and there they prepared to behead him. He knelt, chanting his mantra; the executioner raised his sword, and then a comet flashed across the sky. The swordsman stopped; everyone ran. Nichiren kept chanting. After that, instead of being killed, he was exiled. His life, lived in harmony with the universe, had saved him. His mantra was more than a chant in praise of the Lotus Sutra. Hidden in it, like the diamond in the Gohonzon, was a pattern of sound, a pulsed vibration that was a diagram of the primary forces of the universe. Everyone who chanted it turned into a tuning fork, vibrating in harmony with patterns of energy that filled the space between the stars like music in a concert hall. "At that moment," Andrea said, "I felt completely released from the art I had begun with—the art of an entrapped human soul. What I had revealed was a mirror to the face of the universe."

She had made that mirror out of the most vain, unlikely, and ordinary elements of life: skin lotion, a necklace, prayer beads, bits of carrot, and tar. She called the piece "Tatsunokuchi Beach—Face of the Universe." She stood in the museum and watched while crowds of people looked at it, and while others lingered in front of it, contemplating it, entranced by its intricacy and scale. In a story by Borges, an artist begins to paint a mural of the universe only to discover he has made a picture of his own face. Andrea began, instead, with her face, only to conclude at last that she had made a portrait of the universe.